FOCUS
CONSULTING GROUP INC.

Money, Meaning, and Mindsets:

Radical Reform for the Investment Industry

By Jim Ware
with Keith Robinson and Michael Falk
Foreword by Charles Ellis

CreateSpace Independent Publishing Platform

Design: Fiest Design

Praise for *Money, Meaning, and Mindsets:*

This important and timely book can help every investor correctly define the problem that confronts all investors and will be enormously helpful in figuring out the solution that will work best for each specific investor over the long term.

From the Foreword by Charles Ellis

FCG addresses key issues in this book. Financial services is not the most important industry in America, but it is one that virtually all other industries must depend on. It is the industry that helps to finance our collective growth and much of our innovation. It is too important to all of us to function poorly. We must do better. Trust must be restored. Professionalism must be resurrected. New competition must be both encouraged and challenged. We must earn our keep. We must do more to stand guard against those who operate below a high ethical bar. There is one thing we know for sure, "With regard to morality, markets are always long-term efficient."

Britt Harris, CIO of Texas Teachers Retirement System

FCG puts into words what many in the asset management industry know but few have been willing to acknowledge. We need to get to the point where helping investors achieve better outcomes is valued more highly than winning, and this book is a great framework for helping move the industry in that direction.

Heather Brilliant, CEO, Morningstar Australasia Pty Ltd

In their new book the founders of Focus Consulting Group make it crystal clear that new leadership is required within the asset management industry. Given the enormous challenges the industry is facing we not only need passionate leaders, they need to have a purpose as well. How do we transform from short-term profit for shareholders to long term value creation for all stakeholders? A must read for all investment professionals!

Lars Dijkstra, Chief Investment Officer Kempen Capital Management
and former Chairman of The 300 Club.

Money, Meaning, and Mindsets is a must-read manifesto for those searching for the highest risk adjusted return of all – where purpose and happiness lead to performance. In this seminal book, the authors combine the powerful concept of purpose with its practical application and inject a sense of humor along the way. Enjoy this book's journey that will leave you with a refreshed mind and a renewed will to act.

Suzanne Duncan, Senior Vice President,
Global Head of Research, State Street Global Advisors

FCG has, once again, held up the mirror to our industry for self-reflection. Those who will thrive over the coming years will embrace the imperative of being stewards of client assets and of the capital markets, fighting the headwinds of short-termism and focusing on the efficient deployment of capital to businesses and leaders who can create long term value. This is a call to arms, an opportunity to become even more innovative and impactful. I am confident the industry will emerge stronger from this period of soul searching, with a more sustainable positive impact on clients and their needs."

Michelle R. Seitz, CFA, Head of William Blair Investment Management

FCG's latest book is enlightened, impassioned, persuasive – with the added advantage of being right!

Having worked with FCG for many years, nothing in this wonderful book surprises me – Jim (et al) have preached this gospel forever. (Having worked on Wall Street all my life, nothing about the investment world surprises me.) Few preach this gospel – Jack Bogle being a notable exception.

Ware/Robinson/Falk sound a clarion call for us all to return our business of investing to its rightful position as a profession. For too long we've forgotten our ultimate purpose: investors. If we forget the "value of values" we do so at the peril of our industry. With colorful imagery (literally colorful), the authors make a convincing case that the industry must adapt to stay in the game – and Keynes called it a game. We must prize autonomy, mastery, and purpose among our colleagues, otherwise we won't thrive – and certainly fail to meet the challenges we all face.

With inspirational zeal – almost evangelical zeal – the authors lay down a challenge to our industry. It is now up to us to meet it.

Ted Aronson, CEO of AJO, past Chairman of CFA Institute (then AIMR)

FCG's book, Money, Meaning and Mindsets, exposes the new consciousness to begin to solve the problems that have been created by an industry built on fear and greed.

Lawrence Ford, the shaman of Wall Street
and CEO of Conscious Capital Wealth Management

Money, Meaning and Mindsets provides a healthy and important challenge for the financial industry at a time of ongoing change following a significant financial crisis that has affected it and the global economy in the period from 1997-2008. The financial industry has significant leadership and resourcing challenges as well as having to re-prove that it is truly working in the interests of its clients and the general economy. The only way that the financial industry will address and cope with these challenges is by addressing the cultural and leadership questions raised in this book and asking itself as an industry if it is prepared to adopt these sorts of solutions.

Stefan Dunatov, CIO Coal Pension Trustees Limited,
Chairman of the 300 Club

Money, Meaning, and Mindsets is a wonderful book bringing together many concepts that combine under the headings of "purpose" and "client well-being". It is sad that this will come as new light being shed for too many in our industry but I'm glad you all are leading the charge. The time is perfect for this book as in the 75-plus years since "Where Are the Customers' Yachts" our industry has only become less adept at "wealth care" as you so aptly phrase it.

Dan Davidowitz, CIO, Polen Capital

Money, Meaning, and MIndsets offers a fundamentally new approach for how to think about the investment industry and how to manage investment firms. By focusing on happiness and nobility, the investment industry can shift its reputation from profit to purpose and investment firms can both make money and provide meaning. This outstanding book is relevant, timely, and useful because it not only has a vision of how to manage an investment firm, but also offers specific tools for doing so. Any leader of an investment services firm would be well served to read and apply these ideas.

Dave Ulrich, Rensis Likert Professor,
Ross School of Business, University of Michigan
Partner, The RBL Group

FCG provides a new vision for the Investment Industry; one that aligns with humanity's highest aspirations. If you want to become a successful financial adviser in the 21st century, you must read this book now.

Richard Barrett, Chairman and Founder of the Barrett Values Centre, author of Building a Values-Driven Organization.

What makes this book remarkable is not so much what it says – although that is done superbly – but that what it says needs to be said at all! How did our industry end up getting so much of this wrong after all these years? Hats off to FCG for putting a spotlight on what has been ignored for far too long: just what it means to stand up and call yourself an investment professional.

If we had this book thirty years ago – and made its reading a condition of membership in our "profession", think where our industry could have been today.

Anne Cabot-Alletzhauser, Head, Alexander Forbes Research Institute

Acknowledgments

The partners at Focus Consulting Group (FCG) wish to appreciate our clients over the last two decades. We have learned so much from working with them – lessons of the head and the heart. Only with the ongoing experience of client work, could we have combined theory and practice to produce a compelling vision of the future. We also wish to thank the senior leaders from around the world who come to visit us each year at our Leadership Forum. This opportunity to deepen our connection with these leaders has helped our understanding of the industry considerably (not to mention the good friendships and laughs we've shared.)

Many people have supported FCG and the writing of this book. Their insights and suggestions have been invaluable. In particular, we wish to thank Fred Martin, Suzanne Duncan, Richard Barrett, Charley Ellis, Michael Mauboussin, Paul Smith, Rebecca Fender, Stefan Dunatov, James Valentine, Heather Brilliant, Dave Ulrich, Lars Dijkstra, Britt Harris, Lawrence Ford, John Montgomery, Laura Ercoli, and Liz Severyns. We also thank all our Focus Elite firms, which have set an example for how to do it "right."

Jim Ware: I would like to thank my wonderful wife Jane for allowing the "cave time" it required to research and write the drafts of this book. I am most grateful to my colleagues for their intelligent and heart-felt contributions. I dedicates this book to my children, Alex and Nikki, in the hopes that the financial world will become such a noble calling that they may be drawn to service in it.

Keith Robinson: I would like to acknowledge my FCG teammates and the "Green" leaders in our industry. I continue to learn and grow from our valuable time together. I dedicate this book to my wife, Mary, who "keeps the home fires burning" as I travel the world delivering our message.

Michael Falk: I wish to thank and appreciate my FCG partners for the wonderful dialogues that led to this book, and my clients for the work and experiences that provided so much context. I dedicate this book to my son Collin and his well-being being well-served by a better financial services industry during his life.

We also thank all of our Focus Elite firms: Addenda Capital, AJO, American Beacon Advisors, Disciplined Growth Investors, Forest Investment Associates, Greystone Managed Investments Inc., Kempen Capital Management, Lighthouse Partners, Mawer Investment Management Ltd., Retirement Advisors of America, Roehl & Yi Investment Advisors LLC.

Another group of individuals who have been rich resources for ideas and encouragement are our coaches and strategic partners: Chas Burkhart, Robert Chender, Mary Anne Doggett, David Ellzey, Mike Gasior, Dori Graff, Brooke Graves, Chuck Heisinger, Jane Ingalls, Hank Kinzie, Bryan Kozlowski, Ann Oglanian, Laura Pollock, Bruce Richman, Martha Ringer, Liz Severyns, Jack Skeen, Jody Thompson, Jim Valentine, Jamie Zieglcr.

Foreword

Investors around the world – and most particularly in America – are discovering in increasing numbers that, as investors, they face new challenges that require new ways of defining The Problem and very new ways of figuring out The Solution. This important and timely book can help every investor correctly define the problem that confronts all investors, and will be enormously helpful in figuring out the solution that will work best for each specific investor over the long term.

Years ago, investment management was a judicious combination of a service and a product. The service was investment advice or counsel that helped individuals recognize that each investor is different and so all investors differ as to their objectives. The differences are durable, but do change over time. Major differences include age, wealth, income, prospects for inheritance, interest and skill in investing, risk tolerance, financial responsibilities or obligations, and philanthropic aspirations. With all these variables, it can be no surprise that each of us differs – some or a lot – from every other investor in our personal financial goals and resources. So, of course, what is best for one of us is not best for anyone else. We are unique as investors as we are unique as people, even down to our fingerprints or the iris of our eyes or our DNA.

Once upon a time, centering on each investor's unique objectives for risk avoidance and return achievement, the professional investment advisor crafted a "best fit" definition of that particular investor's optimal investment program and then helped the client stay with the program through the thick and thin of market action.

Then, things changed … gradually at first, but eventually massively. The custom-tailored investment program did not scale. Figuring out the best long-term investment program for each investor took too long, and millions of individuals with moderate savings wanted to invest. So, starting these investors with mutual funds met an increasing need. But change continued, and mutual fund companies rose over the decades in size as profitable businesses. The fund families offered more and more specific mutual funds. With mutual funds expanding to market dominance, investing became a product world. The fund manager defined his or her specialty and offered it to any and all investors as a clearly defined "product." The product concept caught on and, with performance measurement showing how each manager had "performed," most of the money flowed to those managers with the best recent performance in both the individual and institutional parts of the total market. All the vital work of investment counseling and deciding with each client what was best for that client was left to the client to do – alone. To fill the vital void, new firms, called *investment consultants*, were created. But they too soon found that being the manager of managers "scaled" better than custom advice on goals and objectives. So, while they often talked about service, they too tended to drift over to manager selection as a "product." Once again, the individualized service side, for powerful economic reasons all can appreciate, became less and less important.

Meanwhile, fees for investment management rose steadily in two ways that compounded: fee schedules were lifted and lifted again; and, as assets per account or for a whole firm increased substantially, the normal laws of economics did not apply. Managers did not compete for business by lowering fees. As assets managed by firms increased, their fees did not drop nearly as much as would have been the case in other largely fixed-cost businesses. Thus, profits to management firms surged. This history of price stability appears to be unique, particularly for an industry with many competitors, many customers, visible information on fees, performance, and the like, and active intermediaries or advisors offering to help the buyers buy.

Two possible explanations help explain this economic anomaly: Fees are almost never paid directly … in cash or by check. Instead, fees are quietly deducted from the account by the manager, so "out of sight, out of mind" may be at work. Second, by industry custom, fees are defined or calculated in a way that gives all participants – and particularly, clients – the perception that fees are very low: "only 1%." One percent of assets – the assets the investor already has – is, as a percent of the 7% returns that many now expect, close to 15%. That negates the word "only." The next step in recalculating fees is stunning. Since index funds systematically deliver the market rate of return with no more than market-level risk for 0.10%, what more does the investor get from an active manager and how much more does the active manager charge? The answer to the second question is 0.9%, and the answer to the first question is, for the majority of funds, distributing: more risk, more uncertainty, and *less* in returns. Over the past decade, four out of five actively managed mutual funds earned less than the market segment they chose to beat. To put it bluntly, their fees were more than 100% of their "value added."

Active managers as a group, as the corrected data now show, produce a lower-than-market rate of return with a higher-than-market level of risk. So, investors put up all the money and take all the risk and, compared to indexing, absorb less while investment managers are almost the world's highest-paid workers. This presents an existential crisis for active investment managers as individual professionals *and* for their firms, *and* for their industry and for their clients too, *and* for investment consultants.

Turn now, for understanding, to the world of investment management, where enormous changes have combined so forcefully. Of course, participants may well be forgiven if they have not noticed the changes that have come about over more than half a century. (Who would have noticed climate change or the geology that created mountains?) Here are some of the major changes:

- The number of people engaged in active management has increased from less than 5,000 to more than 1,000,000.

- Trading volume on just the New York Stock Exchange (NYSE) has exploded, from 3 million shares a day to more than 3 billion (and derivatives have gone from zero to more than the cash market in value traded).

- The number of Bloomberg terminals has gone from 0 to 320,000.

- The Internet has made everything available to everyone instantly.

- The Securities and Exchange Commission (SEC), via Regulation FD (for "Full Disclosure") requires all public companies to assure that any useful information provided to any one investor is also simultaneously made available to all investors.

- The number of chartered financial analysts (CFAs) has gone from 0 to 120,000 – with more than 200,000 more candidates studying in the queue.

- Securities firms flood the system with data, analysis by experts, and investment advice. Major firms employ as many as 300 experts apiece – experts in each industry, experts in various companies, economists, demographers, political analysts, commodity experts, credit analysts, and portfolio strategists – so it seems fair to say that expertise is now a worldwide "commodity."

- Investment managers in all major countries invest in all major and most other countries around the world.

- Markets are increasingly integrated. Stocks and bonds affect each other and both are affected by the foreign exchange market and by oil. Real estate debt and equity have "gone public" and are traded daily. Gold prices are driven by demand for bullion driven by gold exchange-traded funds (ETFs).

The result of all these equalizing changes is that the old mantra of "beat the market" is terribly misleading. The competition has changed greatly over the past 50 years and this one change may well be more important than any other. Fifty years ago, more than 90% of the NYSE trading was done by individual amateur investors who bought or sold once or twice a year for "outside the market" reasons: a bonus or inheritance received made them a buyer, whereas a home purchase or college tuition bill made them a seller. They had access to almost no investment information. Since then, a nearly complete reversal has transformed the market: more than 95% of trading is done by full-time experts (and some 50% of that is done by the 50 most active experts) working all the time at and for institutional investment organizations. They must buy from each other and must sell to each other because they are the market. Searching everywhere with powerful computers for any market imperfection or pricing error, they strive to make no errors themselves. Well, of course, they do make errors, but can any other investor identify those errors correctly? Not likely, because if they could, they would be famous and we would soon know. And the errors they do make are usually small and do not last, so those small and fleeting mistakes are hard to exploit – and very hard to exploit regularly.

Now, put the two realities together. Fees for active investing are high, very high, and the difficulty of outperforming the expert competition (e.g., the market) is great, very great. The sad result, now documented with hard data, is that active managers are not even keeping up with the market. In fact, more than 80% of actively managed mutual funds fall short of their own chosen objectives – and the shortfalls are bigger than the successes.

So, what should an investor do? First, read this book. In addition, each investor might read Burt Malkiel's *A Random Walk Down Wall Street* (W. W. Norton, 2016) and David Swensen's *Pioneering Portfolio Management* (Free Press, 2009), or even my own *Index Revolution* (Wiley, 2017) or *Winning the Loser's Game* (McGraw-Hill Education, 2017). Second, think through the Great Question raised here (and in the other books cited): If indexing provides a proven process for managing the operations side of investing, can we please return now to the all-important strategic side of investing and concentrate our skills, time, and energy on the long-neglected, but greatly rewarding work of developing for each investor a clear definition of purpose or mission for that specific, unique investor and a long-term investment program most likely to achieve what that investor most wants?

The world of investment management has been, most unfortunately, distorted by the powerful forces of commercial economics. To serve the real needs of investors large and small, it must be rededicated to the great purpose of enabling investors to achieve their realistic and well-considered goals. This is the New Active, which can serve individuals and institutions well and provide inspiring careers for those who care to serve others.

Charles D. Ellis
New Haven, CT

Money, Meaning, and Mindsets:

Radical Reform for the Investment Industry

Jim Ware with Keith Robinson and Michael Falk

CHAPTER ONE

The Invitation: New Mindsets for New Challenges

"The happiness or otherwise of clients is not really relevant."

– Investment professional's statement

T his book invites investment professionals to think differently about the industry. A major premise is Einstein's oft-quoted insight: "We cannot solve our problems with the same thinking used when we created them."[1] Given the general agreement among industry observers – McKinsey, CFA Institute, Casey Quirk, Greenwich, Charley Ellis, Suzanne Duncan, and many others – that we are indeed facing new problems, the time is ripe for a discussion about what Focus Consulting Group (FCG) calls the "New Era."[2] Casey Quirk wrote, "Legacy managers that refuse to change will, over time, see their business erode."[3] FCG surveys reveal that more than 90% of investment professionals agree with this statement.

The current situation may seem a bit frightening, but it is also rich with new possibilities. Investment leaders are asking us, "What is the new landscape? How do we plan and operate in this new world?"[4]

FCG offers its own set of questions:

- What is the purpose of the industry? Why do people want to do investment work?

- How did trust in the investment industry fall so low? Is the low score warranted? How do we win back trust?

- What are the strengths of the investment industry? The weaknesses? The blindspots?

- What is the state of leadership? What must leaders do to succeed in the New Era?

- How will we define and measure success in the New Era?

- How are millennials reshaping the landscape? What is their mindset?

- How do you attract, motivate, develop, and retain talent in the New Era?

- How does the industry shift to incentive systems that reward long-term, positive behaviors?

- What is the role of social investing (ESG, etc.)? Can the industry do well and do good?

These questions suggest that we step back and become curious about the nature of the world we live in and the role of investments. Fortunately, most investors have a natural curiosity, and they tend to be very bright. We can be hopeful that good answers will emerge. Especially if we train ourselves to recognize and use the "Higher Self" – the part of us that is wise, mature, and compassionate – as opposed to the Ego Self, which is fearful and greedy. For too long, the industry has been Ego driven. This book offers a chance to reflect on the future from a mature and thoughtful perspective. What legacy do we want to leave for future generations?

FCG will do its best to reframe these issues in a positive way, and without blaming or preaching. We don't want to appear as Frank Burns in the old *MASH* episodes (millennials, ask your baby boomer colleagues …) where the tone is, "Eat your vegetables," with a healthy dose of finger-wagging. Rather, we'll invite all readers to take responsibility for the state of the industry and ask, "How can we do this differently? How do we bring our wise and compassionate selves to the task of creating an industry that offers real value to all the stakeholders and to the world at large?"

FCG approaches problems from a systems thinking perspective. A *system* is defined as a group of interacting, interrelated, or interdependent elements forming a complex whole.[5] For example, when FCG is invited in to help a firm improve, we avoid the temptation to isolate one team, one process, or one person and then declare, "We've found the problem, and it is John!" Rather, we try to understand the firm, various teams, their processes, their team members, the way the teams interact, the leadership, the strategy, and the culture of the organization. The best results occur when everyone involved takes responsibility for their part in the system, and then asks: "How do we continuously improve?" As we look at the investment industry, we'll use that same approach, rather than trying to lay the blame on someone's doorstep. ("It's the hedge funds!" or "It's the consultants!" or "It's still John.") The systems model that we use in the book is shown in Figure 1.1.

Figure 1.1 Investment Management System

Definition: *A group of interacting, interrelated, or interdependent elements forming a complex whole.*

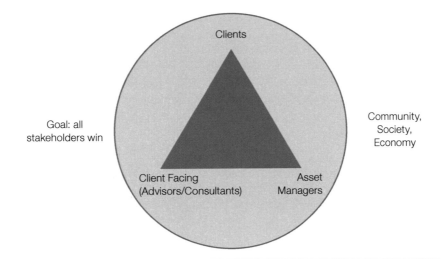

The goal of this exploration is to find a "win" for all the parties involved; that is, the stakeholders. Clients win, the intermediaries meeting with clients win, the asset managers who are investing on behalf of clients win, and the community/society wins.

We define *win* simply as an outcome that provides a sense of well-being for the stakeholder. Note: FCG prefers the term *well-being* to describe the end state. *Well-being* is defined as "the state of being comfortable, healthy, or happy."[6] But for simplicity's sake, we will use the general, more common term *happiness* to describe the end goal that we all are seeking. The point here is to define the end goal for all the people in the investment system shown in Figure 1.1. Common ground or mutual purpose is important to any problem-solving exercise. For the purposes of this book, we'll assume that all parties want to be happy.

Happiness as the Goal of all Goals

FCG suggests that happiness is a good goal because all the participants – clients, asset managers, advisors, consultants, citizens – presumably want to be happy. Aristotle calls happiness the "goal of all goals." Specifically, "Happiness is the meaning and the purpose of life, the whole aim and end of human existence."[7]

Fred Kofman, author of *Conscious Business*, agrees with and elaborates on Aristotle's position:

> *Aristotle called happiness the "highest good" because it is the end of all means. You seek other basic goods such as money, fame, or power because you think they will make you happy, but you want happiness for its own sake. Everything you do – work, play, pray, study, marry, have children – is a search for happiness.*[8]

Let's not quibble over words. If you don't like the word *happiness*, then choose the word you prefer and substitute it: well-being, fulfillment, peace, love, freedom, joy.[9] We'll use *happiness*. We'll also highlight the rather obvious point that being rich does not equal being happy, although many assume that it does. Research on the topic is clear. Nobel Prize winner Daniel Kahneman has studied the money issue and concluded that the benchmark amount in the United States is $75,000. Above that level of income, making more "won't significantly improve your day-to-day happiness."[10]

Already we can hear wailing and protests from some readers: "That's not enough for my happiness! Are you kidding? I live in New York City. I can't even rent an apartment with that income!" Okay. Right. The dollar amount in other cities may be different. Here's the point: People can achieve happiness with far less money than we might otherwise believe. Research on lottery winners shows that indeed they do spike up in happiness after winning giant sums of money … but within 6 months they tend to revert to their original "set point." It turns out happiness is an "inside job." We won't attain high levels of happiness by having more and more wealth. Nevertheless, we certainly won't be happy without a satisfactory level of wealth. And this is the role of the financial world: helping people achieve a satisfactory level.

To add to our discussion of happiness, let's drill a bit further into the psychological underpinnings of happiness. Richard Barrett, in his book, *A New Psychology of Human Well-Being*, writes:

> *Our happiness in life is dependent on being able to master the Ego stages of development (i.e. satisfy our Ego's needs) and our joy is dependent on being able to master the soul stages of development (i.e. satisfy our soul's desires).*[11]

Barrett has taken Abraham Maslow's basic hierarchy model and elaborated on it. Simply put, first we have to take care of basic needs like food, shelter, companionship, and self-esteem before we can then satisfy our higher desires like service, making a difference, and higher purpose. Maslow put it this way: "[F]irst you have to master your deficiency needs before you can fulfill your growth needs."[12] Of course, this is exactly where investments play a vital role. Proper investing helps people to master the deficiency needs. With proper investing and counseling to clients, they can achieve peace of mind about their money issues and move up to what Maslow calls the "growth needs." Make no mistake, the growth needs are the ones that deliver true happiness. A very famous study on happiness is the Harvard Grant study reported by George Vaillant's *Triumphs of Experience*. In the longest study ever conducted on happiness, he found:

> There are two pillars of happiness revealed by the seventy-five-year-old Grant Study. One is love. The other is finding a way of coping with life that does not push love away. The majority of men who flourished found love before thirty and that was why they flourished. ... The seventy-five years and twenty million dollars expended on the Grant Study points, at least, to me, to a straightforward conclusion: "Happiness is love. Full stop. Love conquers all."[13]

Of course, love is not confined to loving another person. We can love many aspects of life: nature, animals, art, work, and causes, to name just a few. Many investment professionals love their work, and for them it is a great source of happiness. Two points to be made here: First, loving the work means just that; it does not mean loving the money you earn. (Ebenezer Scrooge did not appear happy.) There is a big difference in happiness between passion for work and passion for money. In the interview process, we advise clients regularly to look for the former. Studies show that the latter type – so-called "breadheads" – leaves after 18 months for (you guessed it) more money. Second, Albert Schweitzer seems to have it right when he says,

> I don't know what your destiny will be, but one thing I know: the only ones among you who will be really happy are those who will have sought and found how to serve.[14]

Why all this emphasis on happiness? Isn't it obvious that we all want to be happy? So, what's the problem? Many investment professionals don't see the connection between their work and people's happiness. Consider this comment from a client's survey:

> The happiness or otherwise of clients is not really relevant. My job is to protect the financial interests of our clients and generate repeatable returns for appropriate levels of true risk. Everything else is secondary.[15]

This individual does not seem to connect the "financial interests" of the clients with their happiness. Happiness seems to be "secondary." FCG would argue that for the investment industry to serve clients well, we need to elevate happiness to the ultimate goal. We are serving clients to help them achieve financial well-being, which in turn supports their happiness. For example, 71% of married couples claim that money worries contribute to stress in their marriage.[16] Simply put, what's the point of a huge financial industry if it doesn't contribute to the average person's happiness? The same culture report cited in note 15 also yielded this comment from a different employee:

I believe that helping people putting their savings to work and achieving good returns will enable them to live better, happier lives.[17]

This second statement connects "investment success" with "better, happier lives." FCG understands well that no one can *make* another person happy. Providing excellent investment advice and planning does not guarantee that a client will lead a happy life. There are many factors involved. Still, it can be the intention of every investment professional to help clients with what is arguably a huge "happiness" variable: their financial well-being. In FCG's experience, the brilliant minds in the investment world sometimes lose sight of this simple goal. The investment industry must turn its considerable intellectual horsepower toward helping ordinary people solve their financial concerns. Paul Volcker spoke to this issue when he criticized the financial industry by saying that his favorite financial innovation of the past 25 years was the ATM (automated teller machine). Why? "It really helps people. It's useful."[18] In a similarly practical way, we would like to steer the discussion away from markets and benchmarks back to people: to what really helps them achieve happiness or a sense of well-being. The employee quoted earlier (note 17) simply makes the point that achieving good returns (more money) is an *enabler* to live better, happier lives, not a guarantee. It addresses a fundamental fear – loss of security – and helps alleviate it.

Suzanne Duncan (State Street) and Rebecca Fender (CFA Institute) address the disconnect between "investing" and "happiness" by saying that the industry is characterized by "passion without purpose."[19] Investment professionals tend to love their work – and make no mistake, FCG is all about people loving their work. But adding a purpose to their work is critically important. Duncan offers this quote from an asset manager CEO to support her assertion:

People in this industry do not get motivated by creating a better world ... they are interested in returns and competing – nothing else.[20]

Duncan adds, "Many investors view markets as the endgame and lose sight of the fact that markets are just a means to the end of helping clients."[21] As we introduce some new thinking about the industry, we'll explore these concepts and discuss how the industry can connect passion with purpose.

Readers who identify with the earlier quote that "the happiness of clients is not really relevant" may be skeptical about this book. Hang in there. You will find some useful insights even if you don't embrace all aspects of our message. However, we suspect that many readers will be nodding and agreeing that the endgame is happiness: not just for clients, but for shareholders, employees, and all other stakeholders – and for you, the reader.

The real point of this book is to offer different mindsets. We will look at several prevailing mindsets in the investment world and suggest alternatives. We've just examined one such mindset:

Prevailing mindset: beating a benchmark is the goal.

Alternative mindset: helping clients achieve happiness is the goal.

The game is played quite differently depending on which frame you use. Other common mindsets in the investment world include:

- Investing is a zero-sum game (some win, some lose)

- Financial alpha is more relevant than household alpha[22]

- The only purpose of a business is to make a profit (Milton Friedman)[23]

- Compensation drives performance

We'll examine these mindsets, try to understand why they exist, and investigate what mindsets might be more useful for creating a successful and sustainable industry.

We repeat, our goal in writing this book is not to bash or blame investment professionals. Yes, people like Bernie Madoff behaved badly, but he's a statistical outlier. Most investment professionals are hard-working, smart, and well-intentioned. (We know; we work with them weekly.) The trouble is that they are working within a system – the investment industry – that has deeply ingrained mindsets that often lead to suboptimal outcomes. The hedge fund that charges 2 and 20 may believe it is offering superior value. Some do, but the evidence suggests that, on average, hedge funds are not a good value for investors.[24] Most investment professionals have an acute sense of fairness. They can look at situations and quickly see what is fair and what isn't. The trouble comes when they are forced to look at their own value proposition. Then the blinders go on and they have trouble seeing that their firm is not offering value. Back to our original premise on happiness, most investment professionals that we know are not happy when they clearly see that their service adds no value. They truly want to add value. Their intentions are honorable. So, the question becomes, "How might they do that?" This book offers suggestions.

We will introduce and discuss two key models that help explain much of the investment industry's development and why it is struggling. The two models are:

1. Maslow's hierarchy of individual needs. The baby boomer generation, with retirement just ahead, is positioned to move toward the top of the hierarchy: purpose, service, making a difference.

2. Clare Graves's spiral dynamics model of cultural evolution. Many big thinkers[25] have reviewed Graves's model and found it very helpful in explaining human behavior. Graves's model is similar to Maslow's in that both see a pattern to evolution, driven by survival. Graves shows convincingly that different companies and countries have mindsets that influence what people believe and how they behave. The money management industry has clearly operated in one of the mindsets that Graves describes.

These models will help us understand how the investment industry developed and how it may be evolving now. Again, as Einstein observed, it will take a different mindset to solve the current problems.

We'll first examine the current state of the industry before sharing our new thinking. After all, if everything were peachy, there would be no need for change (or a book like this). Few money managers would have looked twice at this book during the 80s or 90s! They were too busy "making money and having fun," as one CEO said to us years ago when asked, "What is the mission of your firm?"

Alas, times have changed. More recently, a CEO said to his senior staff, "The industry is facing a secular decline in profitability." Why is that? And what can be done?

Einstein suggests that new thinking is needed. FCG will offer up some new thinking on where the industry has been, and where it's going.

Summary:

- The investment industry is entering a New Era, with greater competition and lower margins.

- Industry participants are asking, "What's next? What are the guidelines for the New Era?"

- FCG suggests that the industry must address the financial concerns of ordinary people.

- Success looks like integrating theory – Capital Asset Pricing Model and Sharpe ratio – with practice to enhance people's well-being, or simply happiness.

- Two frameworks – Maslow and spiral dynamics – are useful in re-thinking the industry's future.

- A brighter future depends on participants operating from their Higher Selves – wise, mature and compassionate – instead of their Ego selves, motivated by greed and fear.

1   https://www.brainyquote.com/quotes/quotes/a/alberteins121993.html

2   For a copy of FCG's white paper, *The Investment Challenge: Remaining Relevant through Compelling Value* (February 2015), go to our website: www.focuscgroup.com

3   Casey Quirk's white paper, *Life After Benchmarks: Retooling Active Asset Management* (November 2013), http://www.caseyquirk.com/content/whitepapers/Life%20After%20Benchmarks.pdf

4   For simplicity, we'll call the new environment the "New Era."

5   From Merriam-Webster's online dictionary: https://www.merriam-webster.com/dictionary/systems

6   https://www.google.com/#q=definition+of+well-being

7   www.goodreads.com/author/quotes/2192.Aristotle

8   Fred Kofman, *Conscious Business: How to Build Value through Values* (Boulder, CO: Sounds True, 2013), p. 81.

9   *Ibid.*, p. 79.

10 Kevin Short, "Here Is the Income Level at Which Money Won't Make You Happier in Each State," *Huffington Post*, July 25, 2014; http://www.huffingtonpost.com/2014/07/17/map-happiness-benchmark_n_5592194.html

11 Richard Barrett, *A New Psychology of Human Well-Being* (London: lulu.com, 2016), p. 57.

12 Cited in *ibid.*, p. 56.

13 Cited in *ibid.*, p. 58.

14 https://www.brainyquote.com/quotes/quotes/a/albertschw133001.html

15 Written comment from a survey conducted in December 2016, with an FCG client.

16 Suzanne Duncan (State Street Center for Applied Research) and Rebecca Fender (CFA Institute), *Discovering Phi: Motivation as the Hidden Variable of Performance* (October 2016); http://www.statestreet.com/content/dam/statestreet/documents/Articles/CAR/CAR_Phi_Web_FINAL.pdf. Please note that all references to Suzanne Duncan's work are in conjunction with CFA Institute, which partnered on the *Discovering Phi* white paper.

17 *Ibid.*

18 *Wall Street Journal*, December 8, 2009; https://blogs.wsj.com/marketbeat/2009/12/08/volcker-praises-the-atm-blasts-finance-execs-experts/

19 Duncan and Fender, *Discovering Phi*, p. 15. Hereafter, for brevity's sake we'll refer to this partnership simply by lead author Duncan.

20 *Ibid.*

21 Suzanne Duncan, personal telephone communication, January 27, 2017.

22 *Household alpha* is the term used by some investment advisors to describe the value added by advice about taxes, estate planning, financial planning, etc.

23 Friedman's quote seems appropriate for the industrial age, but not so much now.

24 P&I magazine ran a headline on March 6, 2017: "Hedge Funds at the Crossroads: Offer Alpha or Disappear" (Christine Williamson); http://www.pionline.com/article/20170306/PRINT/303069984/firms-at-the-crossroads-offer-alpha-or-disappear. Warren Buffett believes so strongly that hedge funds are a poor value that he bet $1 million on the S&P 500 outperforming any 5 hedge fund portfolio. The results to date: "The fund Buffett picked, Vanguard 500 Index Fund Admiral Shares (which invests in the S&P index), is up 65.67%; Protégé's funds of funds – funds that own a portfolio of positions in a range of hedge funds – are up, on average, a paltry 21.87%."

25 Dr. Clare Graves, *The Never Ending Quest* (ECLET Publishing, 2005). Because spiral dynamics is central to our viewpoint, we emphasize that it is not just one guy's fanciful idea that he thought up after a few beers, but rather a model embraced by scholars such as Ken Wilber, Richard Barrett, Jean Piaget, Kohlberg, Loevinger, Kegan, et al.

CHAPTER TWO

The Investment Industry: From Great to Good

L ong-timers in the industry know that we've enjoyed an incredible ride. It's no wonder that AMG, with great foresight, started buying boutique asset managers years ago. Profitability in the investment industry has been extraordinary. According to Michael Porter, strategy guru, the investment business has been the single most profitable industry:[26]

1. Investments 40.9%

2. Soft drinks 37.6%

3. Prepackaged software 37.6%

4. Pharma 31.7%

5. Perfume, cosmetics 28.6%

It's no surprise that bright people who like puzzles and problem solving – and money – flock to this industry. What does seem a bit surprising is that these same bright people, whose job it is to analyze businesses, can calmly accept the industry's remarkable profitability without raising a skeptical eyebrow. Anyone familiar with Porter's five forces can see in a minute that the investment industry should have, at best, average margins. Why?

- *Are there threats of new entrants?* Yes, every week a new boutique is starting up!

- *Is there intense rivalry* (i.e., lots of competitors)? Heck, yes! (Warren Buffett is on record saying that he hopes competition will help clients "demand lower fees."[27])

- *Do the successful analysts, portfolio managers (PMs), and rainmakers demand high compensation from employers?* For sure!

- *Are there alternatives?* Yes, and they are coming in the form of cheaper delivery systems, lower-priced alternative products, annuities from the insurance industry, and a younger/newer clientele that will search for alternatives to what the industry is offering. (For example, currently the millennial generation has about 50% of their assets in cash.)

So, given these pressures, why have margins been so high for so long? If any industry should mean-revert back to an average level of profitability, it's the investment industry. All the ingredients are there for competition to work its magical invisible hand.

Except one: Pricing structure. Take a holy moment to worship the all-time greatest pricing arrangement ever: fees as a percent of assets. Sheer genius. That pricing structure, which makes the business wonderfully scalable, combined with too little financial literacy on the part of the public (fancy term: *asymmetry of information*) has led to fabulous success.

One can argue that the general public should educate themselves more on financial matters, but the fact is they are largely ignorant of even the basics. A 2016 study asked participants five questions covering aspects of economics and finance encountered in everyday life, such as compound interest, inflation, principles relating to risk and diversification, the relationship between bond prices and interest rates, and the impact that a shorter term can have on total interest payments over the life of a mortgage.[28]

The results? 63% of participants got three or more answers incorrect … out of the five total. When the public is this ill-informed about financial matters, it really behooves investment professionals to take their fiduciary duties seriously. The notion of "buyer beware" is simply not appropriate in this scenario. Interestingly, Tamar Frankel, a fiduciary expert, believes that the ethos and lore of self-reliance in the United States is so strong that despite "asymmetric knowledge," people expect that investment clients should be able to take care of themselves. She writes:

> *Because the vision of the American person as a self-reliant person is paramount, the need for law or for government to protect clients is weakened – Americans can take care of themselves as against their fiduciaries.*[29]

We'll have more to say on fiduciary duties in Chapter 8, "Blindspots."

Hence, we've had a case of the foxes guarding the henhouse. We'll get into this more in the following chapters when we discuss mindsets. Again, we're not casting blame or shame on the foxes: They are beautiful animals, doing what they were intended to do. But if you put them in charge of the henhouse, well, predictable things happen. Foxes like their chickens. Investment pros like their income. Not complicated.

It's been a great run for the foxes, with decades of good spoils. Combine a big bull market – since the average baby boomer came of age – with a heavenly pricing scheme and an asymmetry of information and wonderful things happen. But now the industry is finally beginning to respond to economic forces. Good times can't last forever. McKinsey writes, "The North American asset management industry is on the brink of a once-in-a-generation shift in competitive dynamics … [and] the end of 30 years of exceptional investment returns."[30] Take another appreciative moment to realize how lucky we've all been as participants in this industry.[31]

However, it's changing. The so-called asymmetry of information is shrinking or at least shifting, partly due to the ease and inexpensive fees of index funds. The media and industry pundits like Charley Ellis and Jack Bogle continue to aggressively educate the population about the realities of the investment industry. As a result, a recent piece from the Center for Applied Research (State Street) and CFA Institute found that "46% of institutional investors believe the fees they pay are not commensurate with the value that is delivered."[32] On the retail side, 54% of clients agreed that "the investment advice most financial advisors offer is not worth 1% of the investor's account value that many charge."[33] Michael Goldstein provides perspective on these fees in this statement:

Thirty years ago the largest brokerage firms generated 100 basis points of revenue on each dollar of retail assets held in custody, 10% of the Treasury Bond yield. Now their fees average around 70 basis points, more than a third of the Bond's yield.[34]

Goldstein thus argues that industry pricing is even higher now, and therefore the value to investment clients is lower. He's also all over the symmetry argument, saying "Confusion is generally more profitable than clarity."[35]

In a *Wall Street Journal* piece titled, *"It's Time for Investor Fees to Go Even Lower,"* journalist Jason Zweig writes,

That so-called fulcrum fee helps put fund managers on the same side of the table as you. When you make more money, their fee goes up; when you make less, their fee goes down.

But managers overwhelmingly prefer charging flat fees that aren't tied to returns. Only 211 stock or bond mutual funds with a combined $996 billion in assets, out of a grand total of 7,621 funds with $13.8 trillion in assets, charge performance-based fees, according to Jeff Tjornehoj of Broadridge Financial Solutions in Denver. That's fewer than one in 36 funds, and less than $1 out of every $14 in total assets.

And that isn't progress. Back in 1972, the Securities and Exchange Commission reported that 103 out of 999 funds, or more than 10%, were charging fulcrum fees.[36]

A simple way to describe the value proposition offered by many active managers is: They are selling Timex watches at Rolex prices. For the record, FCG believes in active management. There are good active managers who deserve their higher fees. But active managers as a whole aren't delivering. (By definition, they can't: it's a zero-sum game, and worse after fees.)

We've all seen the studies on shrinking alpha. The industry "still spends 60% of its capital on the pursuit of alpha … even though alpha opportunities are becoming increasingly rare."[37]

How rare?

According to researchers at the University of Maryland, prior to 1990, 14 percent of US domestic equity mutual funds were delivering "true" alpha. "True" alpha in this case was identified by using statistical methods to single out funds where performance above their respective benchmarks couldn't be explained by probability alone. By 2006, however, the percentage of funds delivering "true" alpha had shrunk to only 0.6 percent, while the total number of actively number of actively managed funds had increased 5x. This isn't just a US phenomenon. Alpha production net of fees is difficult across the globe."[38]

Larry Swedroe offers corroborating data. He claims that there are far fewer active managers who can deliver alpha than there were 20 years ago:

The portion able to do so has dropped from about 20% to about 2%, and that's even before considering the impact of taxes. For taxable investors, the largest cost of active management is often taxes, so the 2% figure should probably be cut in half. A 1% chance of success isn't very good odds, which is why there's been a persistent trend by both individual and institutional investors away from active toward passive management.[39]

In most industries, more competition means a better deal for the consumer. But that's not so in the investment industry. In our industry, more excellent competitors simply means it is harder for any of them to win consistently. However, fee competition does benefit the client, and that form of competition is on the rise.

No wonder the average person doesn't find value in traditional active firms. As a result, they are leaving active managers in droves. As Burton Malkiel writes, "Year after year, when results come in, low-cost index funds prove their worth as the optimal way to invest."[40] He recommends, "Everyone should use index funds as the core of their investment portfolios."[41]

Michael Mauboussin at Credit Suisse uses a poker analogy to explain why alpha is scarce:

Investors are shifting their investment allocations from active to passive management. This trend has accelerated in recent years. The investors who are shifting from active to passive are less informed than those who stay. This is equivalent to the weak players leaving the poker table. Since the winners need losers, this can make the market even more efficient, and hence less attractive, for those who remain. If you can't identify the patsy, or weak player, it's probably you.[42]

Clients are waking up to the value disparity, and the industry is under pressure. We know this from the Edelman Trust Barometer, which currently ranks the investment industry near the bottom of all industries. Here are the responses for the survey question, "How much do you trust businesses in each of the following industries to do what is right?"[43]

1. Technology 77%
2. Food & beverage 68%
3. Brewing & spirits 65%
4. Pharmaceuticals 64%
5. Telecommunications 62%
6. Consumer packaged goods 62%
7. Energy 62%
8. Automotive 60%
9. Entertainment 55%
10. Financial services 51%
11. Media 47%

Additional details from the report are not comforting:

- For readers taking refuge in the fact that financial services and banks are giant industries, we're sorry to inform you that the breakouts don't improve the picture. Financial Advisory/Asset Management ranks worse than banks or credit cards. (Insurance ranks worst of all.)

- The informed public believes that "Greed/Money" ranks higher as a motivator than "Improve People's Lives" or "Make the World a Better Place" (54% vs. 30% and 24%, respectively).

- Worse yet, because of the deep distrust of financial service firms, the informed public believes that much more regulation is needed for financial service firms. (54% say that government needs to regulate financial services *more*. Ouch.)

- When asked what behaviors are important to building trust, these behaviors were top-rated:
    - Ensures quality control
    - Keeps me and my family safe
    - Embraces sustainable business practices
    - Is transparent in reporting progress on company's social responsibilities

- For the preceding factors, the informed public does not believe that financial services companies are performing well on them. (The gap between "Importance of behavior" and "Performance on behavior" was more than 25% for each.)

The public doesn't perceive that asset managers are "doing right" by them. Looking at the preceding list of industries, the rankings make intuitive sense. We own iPhones and they work well. Same with our laptops. Food and beverage? We shop at local grocery stores and get good products at reasonable prices. And so on, down the list. From a value perspective, most of these industries deliver to society at large. But what about the investment industry? If our job is to solve investment issues for people, then many observers would claim we've failed. There seems to be a gross disconnect between the financial well-being of the investment professionals and their clients in aggregate. Specifically, only 21% of U.S. citizens are "very confident" they will have enough money to retire. More importantly, when we dive deeper into the assumptions for that very confident group, we find:[44]

- 14% of them were not saving at all!

- 33% of them had less than $50,000 in savings.

- 30% had never estimated how much they need.

Shocking, right? And this group was very confident. This picture would be the medical equivalent of nearly all of us suffering from various forms of cancer, but being very confident about our long-term health.[45]

Another expert source on retirement reports:

The Economic Policy Institute notes that the average retirement savings for all U.S. families is just $95,776. As low as that number seems, it exaggerates the broader health of retirement savings because some high savers skew the figures;

the median (those in the middle of the pack) for families with any retirement savings is $60,000 and for all families is just $5,000. Nearly half of the working-age families have no savings at all for retirement, according to the institute.[46]

As one investment expert expressed it, "It's quite amazing. If automobile firms manufactured cars that routinely broke down, they'd be out of business. So, why is it that the investment industry which clearly has not prepared the public for retirement can stay in business?" Another investment professional glibly responded, "It's hard to kill asset management firms."

When we shared the Edelman data with Fred Martin, CEO of Disciplined Growth Investors, he responded:

Frankly, I do not need a survey to tell me the perilous state of investment management relationships. I see the problems every day:

1) *Last month I looked over the portfolio of a friend. His portfolio included at least fifty mutual funds. Nowadays most mutual funds own 200 or more stocks in each fund. He most likely owns 2000 or more stocks. His portfolio has become a de facto index fund, but he is paying investment management fees far in excess of index fund fees.*

2) *Three years ago, I attended an industry conference for CEOs only. Their solution to the lousy performance results achieved since 2008? Create more complex products that nobody understands. Target date funds? Liquid alts? Smart Beta? Can anyone define their usefulness in one sentence?*

3) *In 2007, the year before we met, my wife purchased a variable annuity. She has never changed the investments in her annuity. Nine years later, her variable annuity is below her initial cost, while the S&P 500 is up more than 60%, including dividends. It took me a whole year and numerous phone calls to find out her annual fees, a whopping 3% per year. No wonder she has lost money.*

4) *In 2003 my firm was hired by a Fortune 100 firm to manage a small-cap growth portfolio. After one quarter's outperformance they doubled the assets under our care. During the next quarter, we underperformed the benchmark. The client fired us. The story gets worse. Three years ago, the same company approached us to manage a portion of their pension fund. We told them the sorry story of our prior association with their company. We insisted that, if they hired us, they would treat us as a long-term investor. They told us they had completely changed personnel and wanted a long-term relationship. Within six months they had cut the funds with us in half; three months later they fired us. I grieve for the*

shareholders and beneficiaries of that schizophrenic company. My sales guy is still humiliated, because he went to bat for this customer and assured us that the prospect had reformed. That company will never again be a customer of our firm. Ever.

5) *Last year we conducted focus group sessions with individual investors. None of the 24 participants were customers; all had some investment assets. Not a single participant knew what they were spending on their total annual investment management expenses.*

Is it any wonder that unreasonable fees and investment practices are rampant? Is it any wonder why our industry has such low trust scores?

Two recent events have made the situation even worse. In 2007, social media began to become a key part of the communications system. This new technology created a new pathway to transparency. In 2008, the financial system nearly collapsed. In my opinion 2008 was a watershed year, ending the bull market in financial assets which began in 1982. 2008 was a deeply frightening year. Far too many investors succumbed to the fear by selling a high-return asset class (stocks) and buying a low-return asset class (bonds). Eight years later those decisions have proven terribly misguided. Yet most investors are still over-invested in bonds.

Investment managers have not yet recovered from 2008. Instead of focusing on helping their clients make wise decisions after 2008, they still try to beat their benchmark with increasingly futile results. They continue to trade their portfolios wildly; many mutual funds report turnover exceeding 100% per year! These trades benefit the brokerage industry, NOT the client.[47]

The real question here seems to be value. Whether it's buying laptops or groceries or autos, we want to get a fair deal. When it comes to investment decisions, most clients have only the basic tools for understanding services provided. Financial literacy remains shockingly low around the world. The average consumer does not understand how interest rates affect bond prices, what "growth" stocks are, or even the difference between common stock and livestock. They know as little about the workings of investments as most of us know about car engines. If the investment industry wants to establish itself as a trusted industry, then it must communicate more clearly and objectively. Consider the happiness (read: well-being) of the clients. Assume they know very little about the inner workings of markets and instead talk outcomes with them. Don't make them feel stupid or helpless. Raise and address key basic issues:

• How much do they want to live on when they retire?

• How much insurance do they need?

- What will it cost to educate their children?

- How does a basic financial plan work?

Many advisory firms still don't promote an understanding of these key basic issues. It's humorous to read the typical advisor letter to clients. Here's a sampling:

> *U.S. interest rates are likely to remain lower-for-longer even if there will be temporary spikes in yields. The U.S. economy is arguably the strongest in the world today yet our interest rates are relatively high as compared to other developed economies globally, the weaknesses in our primary overseas trade partners' economies and the possibility of a recession in the next two years possible. Bonds are certainly not cheap, but the prevailing opinions that they are uniformly dangerous are overblown.[48]*

Client reaction: "Huh?" (Followed by, "Is this supposed to mean something to me?")

Seriously. Do the advisors think that their clients get ANY value from this? The quoted letter illustrates a well-studied phenomenon called the "Curse of Knowledge":

> *Once we know something, we find it hard to imagine what it was like not to know it. Our knowledge has "cursed" us. And it becomes difficult for us to share our knowledge with others, because we can't readily re-create our listeners' state of mind.[49]*

If the investment industry really want to help the average person become happier about finances, they should stop talking gibberish. Once Jim asked a senior executive at a large New York City pension manager why the language in the industry was so complicated. Within minutes he had lost Jim in a barrage of impenetrable concepts and words. Jim smiled and thought, "This is exactly the problem." The Curse of Knowledge. But remember, confusion is generally more profitable than clarity. There's method to the madness.

So, what is the proper role of the investment industry? Co-author Michael Falk suggests the following: an investment professional should strive to positively impact the financial lives of as many people as possible[50] – and by so doing, make their lives in general better. Less worry about finances, fewer marital fights over money, better night's sleep knowing that they have a plan in place, the reassurance that someone who knows investments will take care of them. A financial advisor looks after your financial well-being as a doctor looks after your physical well-being. Each of them helps you understand the part you must play. Doctors encourage you to stop smoking, eat right, get regular physical check-ups, and so on. A financial advisor helps you articulate your goals, develop an investment plan, and learn to stick with it. In neither case does the professional expect the client to become an expert. (At one conference, a participant asserted that the problems outlined earlier in this chapter were the client's fault for not understanding investments. Hence, the client was not taking responsibility! Excuse us, but isn't that the idea behind being a *fiduciary*?!)

So, what went wrong? In our view, the brilliant investment minds in the business had so much fun doing the work, and making piles of money, that they seemingly lost track of the industry's purpose: to help people. In fact, many investment CEOs and CIOs cannot offer a compelling statement of purpose. One CIO started an offsite session with his investment team by showing a short clip of Simon Sinek discussing the premise of his book, *Start with Why*.[51] It's a good clip in which Sinek makes his basic point that purpose motivates people and drives success. He makes many of the same points that Collins makes in *Built to Last*.[52] At the end of the clip, the CIO said a few words about it and then prepared to move on. Jim asked a logical follow-up question, "So, what is your team's purpose?" To his credit, the CIO was very candid and responded, "I don't know. I'm working on it."

This CIO is not alone. A survey by State Street Global Advisors asked professionals to what degree their work reflects their values and mission in life. The result? "Financial services ranked 12th out of 13 industries."[53]

Ellis writes, "Investment professionals have falsely defined their professional mission to clients and prospective clients as beating the market."[54] The consulting firm Casey Quirk agrees and has written a report called *Life after Benchmarks*.[55] Suzanne Duncan summarizes it well: "The client IS the benchmark."[56]

We'll get more into purpose later, but the point here is simple. Purpose becomes less important in a bull market when everyone is profiting handsomely. In the 90s, one CEO at a very successful firm said that his firm's purpose was to "have fun and make money, in that order." Notice that there is nothing in his statement about serving clients!

Well, the client is actively (pun intended) entering the picture. The investment industry now must face a hard business truth: You must provide value to remain relevant. Clients are voting with their feet and leaving active managers in droves. The Vanguard Group, famous for its passive strategies (indexing), "now controls more in retail monies, taken in directly and through advisors, than any of the leading brokerage firms."[57]

With fees compressing, profit margins shrinking, alpha less dependable, ever-greater regulation,[58] digital alternatives, millennial mindsets, and money flowing to cheap index funds, the investment industry is indeed ripe for some new thinking – and we do mean new thinking. One major consulting firm talks about a "willingness to question old orthodoxies" and then proceeds to trot out all the usual suspects as hope for the future. For example, the "new value propositions will require robust new capabilities … like asset allocation over security selection … and delivery of alpha and client service."

Puh-lease. Keith and Jim both worked for Gary Brinson, who wrote a famous paper on the value of asset allocation versus security selection and made it a strategic cornerstone of Brinson Partners 30 years ago.[59] And "delivery of alpha and client service"? Isn't that exactly the model that active firms have allegedly been using for decades?

Don't misunderstand: The big consulting firms provide great data, but they fall in line pretty quickly when it comes to challenging the old orthodoxies. We understand the behavioral implications for career risk.

With this brief review of the state of the industry, let's move to the models we mentioned earlier. They provide a framework for understanding how the industry developed and where it might constructively go.

Remember, the big mindset shift so far is aiming for client happiness over an abstract concept like "beating a benchmark." The best firms we know have photos of their clients in the entryway, and bring those clients in frequently to talk to staff members. They know their clients and what makes them happy.

Summary:

- The extraordinary profitability of the investment industry is in secular decline.

- The fox has been in charge of the henhouse.

- Increasingly, clients are insisting on added value for active fees.

- Alpha is scarce; money is moving to passive funds.

- Edelman's Trust Barometer shows very low trust scores for the investment industry.

- The "crisis" in the industry provides an opportunity to re-think the future.

- New mindsets are needed to meet today's challenges.

---

26   Michael Porter, "Five Competitive Forces That Shape Industry," *Harvard Business Review* (January 2008); https://hbr.org/2008/01/the-five-competitive-forces-that-shape-strategy. Figures shown are profit margins.

27   Jason Zweig, "It's Time for Investor Fees to Go Even Lower," *Wall Street Journal* (January 6, 2017); https://blogs.wsj.com/moneybeat/2017/01/06/its-time-for-investor-fees-to-go-even-lower/

28   www.usfinancialcapability.org/

29   Tamar Frankel, *Fiduciary Law* (New York: Oxford University Press, 2010), p. xiv.

30   McKinsey & Company report, *Thriving in the New Abnormal* (November 2016), p. 1; http://www.mckinsey.com/industries/financial-services/our-insights/thriving-in-the-new-abnormal-north-american-asset-management

31   My partners and I understand that we charge higher consulting fees than those in other industries. (But less than many in OUR industry!) So, we have benefited from the profitability of the investment world. That's not a blindspot for us!

[32] Suzanne Duncan, State Street Center for Applied Research, *Influential Investor* (November 2012), p. 15; http://www.statestreet.com/content/dam/statestreet/documents/Articles/CAR/InfluentialInvestor_report.pdf

[33] BNY Mellon report, *Third Annual Study of Advisory Success* (June 2015), p. 11; https://www.pershing.com/_global-assets/pdf/third-annual-study-of-advisory-success.pdf

[34] Michael Goldstein, FMMI Inc. (November 7, 2016), p. 2.

[35] *Ibid.*, p. 6.

[36] Jason Zweig, "It's Time for Investor Fees to Go Even Lower," *Wall Street Journal* (January 6, 2017); https://blogs.wsj.com/moneybeat/2017/01/06/its-time-for-investor-fees-to-go-even-lower/

[37] Suzanne Duncan, State Street Center for Applied Research, *The Folklore of Finance* (2014), p. 5.

[38] Suzanne Duncan, *The Folklore of Finance*, p. 6.

[39] Larry Swedroe, "New Evidence that Challenges Active Management," *Advisor Perspectives* (December 21, 2016).

[40] Burton Malkiel, "Foreword," in Charley Ellis, *The Index Revolution* (Hoboken, NJ: John Wiley & Sons, 2016), p. viii.

[41] *Ibid.*, p. vii.

[42] Michael Mauboussin, Credit Suisse report "Looking for Easy Games," (January 4, 2017), p. 2.

[43] https://www.cfainstitute.org/learning/future/getinvolved/Documents/trust_to_loyalty_executive_summary.pdf

[44] Michael Falk, from his CFA retirement lecture based on 2016 EBRI Retirement Confidence Survey data, delivered to CFA audiences around the world. Mr. Falk is the author of a book from the Research Foundation of the CFA Institute on entitlements and their impact on the sustainability of long term growth. The title is *Let's All Learn How to Fish...to sustain long-term economic growth.* For more, see www.letsalllearnhowtofish.com

[45] Employee Benefit Research Institute, 2016 Retirement Conference Survey.

[46] *Barron's* (January 7, 2017).

[47] Fred Martin, personal email communication, January 17, 2017.

[48] Financial letter from an advisor firm.

[49] Heath & Heath, *Made to Stick* (New York: Random House, 2007), p. 20.

[50] Thanks to Michael Falk on our team for this simple but powerful purpose statement, which he lives.

[51] Simon Sinek, *Start with Why* (New York: Penguin Group, 2011). To view the clip, go to YouTube: https://www.youtube.com/watch?v=IPYeCltXpxw

[52] Jim Collins, *Built to Last* (New York: HarperCollins, 2002).

[53] Duncan, *Discovering Phi*, p. 27. Only retail ranked lower.

[54] *Ibid.*, 131.

[55] Casey Quirk, *Life after Benchmarks*.

[56] Duncan, *Folklore of Finance*, p. 12.

[57] Goldstein, FMMI report, page 6.

[58] As with government, we get the regulation we deserve.

[59] https://scholar.google.com/scholar?q=brinson+hood+beebower+asset+allocation&hl=en&as_sdt=0&as_vis=1&oi=scholart&sa=X&ved=0ahUKEwjOtNXl2K7RAhVn7YMKHRN-CfMQgQMIGDAA

CHAPTER THREE

New Mindsets for Envisioning the Future: Maslow

T he first model that we are keen to introduce allows a different framing of the future. If we acknowledge that the "old" thinking is unlikely to solve today's issues, then perhaps some new thinking will. Maslow's hierarchy of needs, adjusted slightly by Richard Barrett for corporate use, offers insights.[60]

Maslow's model is straightforward, and many investment professionals know the basics, shown in Figure 3.1.

Figure 3.1 Maslow's hierarchy of needs

Self-Actualization

Purpose, Service, Connection

Growth Needs
When these needs are fulfilled, they do not go away; rather, they engender deeper levels of motivation and commitment.

Self-Esteem

Love & Belonging

Safety

Physiological

Deficiency Needs
An individual gains no sense of lasting satisfaction from being able to meet these needs, but feels a sense of anxiety if these needs are not met.

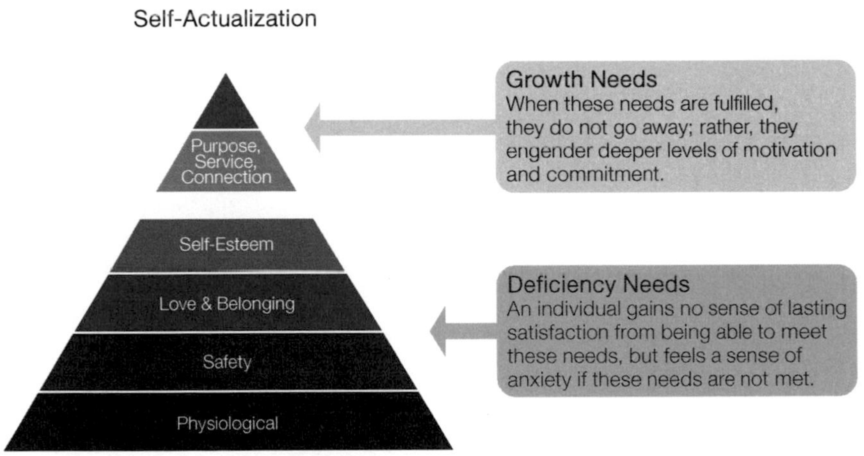

The model makes intuitive sense. All of us start at the bottom and work our way up as needs are fulfilled. First, we satisfy basic physical needs: warmth, shelter, food, clothing, etc. Second, we need to feel safe from attack and various dangers. As these primal needs get met, then we naturally want to belong and have connection with others. Finally, when all these needs are met, we begin to look for ways to excel and show mastery. These are self-esteem needs, the fulfillment of which builds confidence.

The less common aspect of the model is where it gets interesting and useful for our exploration of an investment future. For example, at the lower "red" levels, our main concern is fear. We are afraid for our safety, for our approval by others, and for our security around competence. In our work with clients, FCG simplifies the red territory by saying it is the "fear zone" or "under the line" territory. The three big fears are:[62]

1. Loss of security/safety

2. Loss of approval

3. Loss of control

On any given day, we may get triggered by any one or all of these fears. For example, if you are driving to work and hit a patch of ice which sends your car swerving, you immediately feel a loss of safety. You might crash. Adrenaline pumps through your system, as your heart races. You probably utter some choice words. With luck, you regain control of the car, your body returns to normal functioning, and on you go.

Loss of approval shows up at work during a discussion when you withhold your ideas because people may not like them. You want to say something brilliant that will create enthusiasm and head-nodding, but you are afraid that instead people may look at you funny. You want your ideas to be well received; you are afraid they won't be. Loss of approval (more specifically, the *fear* of loss of approval) might keep you silent.

Loss of control might involve decision rights. For example, there is an important project being initiated, one that you care deeply about. You want to lead the project because you have confidence you can deliver a fine outcome. You may feel anxious that someone else will get to lead the project, and you will suffer loss of control. It would become their baby, not yours.

Any time you feel a little bit upset at work, you can usually trace the upset back to one of these three big fears, all of which fit nicely into the Maslow hierarchy.

For our client work, we've created a map of the territory, shown in Figure 3.2.

Figure 3.2

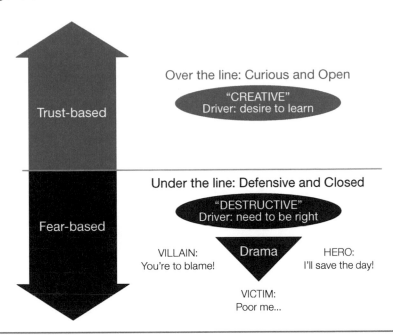

Many firms have found this graphic to be simple but helpful. Einstein believed, "No model is perfect, but some are useful." Clients find this one very useful. When discussions go badly, and drama erupts, this model provides a quick way to analyze what happened. Drama occurs when one or more participants get triggered (become fearful in some way) and then drop under the line. At this point, the conversation becomes defensive and less productive. Participants typically assume one of three personas – "masks" – which are:

- **Villain:** blaming others, attacking, taking no responsibility

- **Victim:** poor me, submissive, also takes no responsibility

- **Hero:** over-functioning to save the day; micromanaging, takes too much responsibility, suppresses learning

As teams become more sophisticated in their discussions, they learn to recognize when one or more participants has dropped under the line. Instead of continuing from the same consciousness, smart teams call it out, and then take a constructive action, such as breaking for five minutes. Alternatively, they could address the situation directly by asking, "What happened?", invoking curiosity rather than defensiveness.

High-performing teams at Google discovered that the characteristic they all shared was "psychological safety."[63] Psychological safety manifests when teams are trusting and respectful of one another, and minimize the time spent "under the line." Understanding the model in Figure 3.2 and becoming increasingly skilled at staying over the line pays huge dividends for teams whose value involves decision making. Thinking improves when we are free of fear. Maslow would counsel us to strengthen our internal sense of confidence around security/safety, approval/belonging, and control/mastery. How? Begin to notice when you get triggered and learn to (1) observe it, and (2) let it go. Invoke your Higher Self. As a team gains confidence in these lower "deficiency needs," it begins to perform better. Most of the time, a disruptive team member – which FCG has labeled a "Red X" – is falling prey to these deficiency needs and responding with under-the-line behaviors: blaming, gossiping, controlling. Maslow's straightforward model helps us to identify and address these behaviors.

FCG clients who master this skill of operating predominantly over the line tend to outperform. Suzanne Duncan at State Street has researched this phenomenon in the investment world. Her findings add considerable weight to the experience FCG has had with clients. Specifically, her research has identified a hidden variable that she calls "phi," defined as "a type of motivation stemming from an internalized purpose that fosters the most important factors of performance."[63]

FCG advises investment professionals to master their Maslow deficiency needs sufficiently, so that they can focus their attention on "phi," which is in the upper area of Maslow's hierarchy: purpose, meaning, making a difference. The results are remarkable for investment professionals who do this:

A one-point increase in phi is associated with:

• 28% greater odds of excellent long-term organizational performance

• 55% greater odds of excellent client satisfaction

• 57% greater odds of excellent employee engagement[64]

Much of Duncan's research dovetails nicely with Daniel Pink's work on motivation[65] for knowledge professionals. They both agree that these factors lead to intrinsic and sustainable motivation:

• Purpose: articulating a compelling reason for why the work is important, such as helping clients fulfill their goals

• Mastery: steady progress toward greater excellence in one's expertise

• Autonomy: freedom to do the work as one chooses

Importantly, both Duncan and Pink discount the effectiveness of extrinsic motivators such as money. In the Maslow framework, both Duncan and Pink are pointing toward the top of the pyramid, suggesting to investment leaders that increased happiness and effectiveness of staff members will be achieved by focusing on these intrinsic motivators, the "phi."

As mentioned earlier, Duncan says that the investment industry is high in passion, but low in purpose. FCG can support this claim with its own research on more than 2,000 investment professionals. When asked what motivates them, investment professionals respond as shown in Figure 3.3.

Figure 3.3 Please choose the two factors that are the most meaningful in your daily experience

The work serves a larger purpose, doing something positive in the world (such as allocating capital property in the markets.)	**8%**
The work contributes to a sound and sustainable financial future for our firm.	**15%**
The work benefits our clients, and I enjoy happy clients most of all about my job	**23%**
The work allows me to spend time with bright and engaging colleagues. I like these team interactions best of all.	**22%**
The work is interesting, challenging and intellectually stimulating.	**32%**

As Duncan states, the high vote-getter is passion for the work, and the low vote-getter is purpose. Similarly, in her research, Duncan found that "just 17% of our respondents said they joined the investment management industry for this larger purpose of helping clients achieving financial goals, and only 6% said they joined to contribute to economic growth."[66]

So, what is driving this disconnection from the industry's larger purpose? Duncan writes, "Quite simply, the environment we ourselves have created to support our passion prevents our connection to the very purpose that could focus that passion, and drive the performance we seek." Interestingly, Ellis makes a similar point in his latest book:

Talented, competitive people attracted to investment management have, however unintentionally, gotten so caught up in competing for the tangible prizes that they are not asking potentially disruptive questions about the real value of their best efforts.[67]

In a presentation to investment leaders from 34 different firms, all of the attendees responded positively to a polling question that asked, "Is having a sense of purpose important to your firm's future success?" But when asked a follow-up question, "Do you find the purpose statement of your firm compelling?" they responded as shown in Figure 3.4.

Figure 3.4 I find the purpose statement of our firm compelling. (Why, not What)

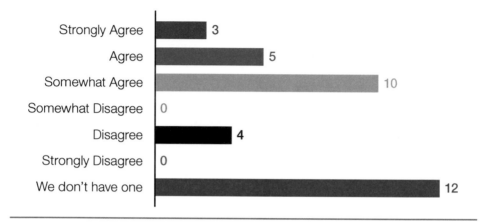

Only three leaders said that their firm had a compelling "why" for their business. Twelve leaders said that their firm did not have one at all![68]

In the New Era for the industry, a wonderful opportunity exists for leaders to focus on purpose as a motivator. That is exactly what Maslow's hierarchy suggests: once we have satisfied our basic deficiency needs (safety, connection, self-esteem), we naturally aspire to the higher growth needs: service, purpose, making a difference. Yet, Duncan's research shows that "only 44% of professional investors believe that their leaders articulate a compelling vision, and just 41% agree that leaders talk to employees about their most important values and beliefs."[69]

Duncan goes on to state that investment leaders' lack of skill around leading from purpose ultimately "drives demotivation and stress. Consequently, 84% of all investment professionals report being demotivated in some way, and 68% reported having medical issues as a result of stress."[70] It's remarkable that people working in an industry that is both fascinating and wildly profitable would feel demotivated and experience stress-related physical issues. Something is wrong. We'll spend more time exploring that in later chapters, but one significant factor is that the industry keeps score.

Success reinforced by extrinsic motivators, like money, drives us to pay more attention to the lower levels of the hierarchy because that's how the industry has defined winning. This is not a surprise, but it is a difficult cycle to break.

In FCG's over-/under-the-line model, Ego operates under the line. Our Ego's job is to navigate in the world and keep us safe and alive. Ego only knows survival and shows up in the investment world prominently as fear and greed. We call people who are excessively greedy or selfish "Ego-driven." So, the big challenge for leaders is to understand and manage the employee Egos so that the achievement of security, relationship, and self-esteem takes place in a healthy way. Note: The goal is not to eliminate the Ego, because that is not realistic. The Ego serves a purpose: navigating the lower needs. However, the Ego doesn't understand the higher levels of consciousness in the model – ethics, larger purpose, social responsibility – so good leaders must help workers transform from a fear-based (Ego) mentality to a growth (Higher Self, Mature Self, Soul) mentality. The best firms that FCG works with have moved into this consciousness where they are driven more by growth needs than by deficiency needs.

Maslow's hierarchy of needs provides a solid blueprint for moving beyond deficiency needs (which are Ego-driven) and up into the growth needs, which provide a more lasting sense of happiness or well-being. Our industry is often characterized as "ego intensive." Ego and competition usually go hand in hand. Show us a roomful of competitive people, strutting their stuff, and we'll show you a lot of Egos on display. But as investment professionals age and mature, there is a natural movement toward the higher levels of Maslow's hierarchy. If given a nudge, many of those people will focus on their growth needs, like purpose and service, and start reaping the benefits of Duncan's phi factor. The obstacle to this natural evolution is the excitement and challenge of the investment world. Many investment leaders remain focused on competing and winning – the adrenaline rush – to the exclusion of moving up the hierarchy. In FCG's experience, we have seen very positive results just by bringing this choice to the attention of leaders. It's a natural evolution, so it doesn't take much arm-twisting. Maslow points the way to a very promising movement from "passion-only" to "passion and purpose": from a mindset steeped in competition to one that is balanced with service.

Maslow provides a positive frame for the individual. Let's next move to a model that provides a positive frame for the whole industry.

Summary:

- Maslow's hierarchy-of-needs model indicates that people are motivated by deficiency needs and growth needs.

- When people have met their deficiency needs – safety, belonging, and self-esteem – they naturally aspire to meet their growth needs: purpose, service, greater good.

- Our Ego aims to satisfy our deficiency needs, whereas our Higher Self is motivated by growth needs.

- The investment industry seems largely motivated by Ego, as evidenced by the absence of purpose-driven companies in Duncan's research at State Street.

- The industry is poised to move from "passion driven" to both "passion and purpose driven."

---

60 Richard Barrett, *The Values Driven Organization* (New York: Routledge, 2014).

61 For more on this model, see Hale Dwoskin's book, *The Sedona Method* (Sedona, AZ: Sedona Press, 2007).

62 Charles Duhig, "What Google Learned from Its Quest to Build the Perfect Team," *New York Times Magazine*, February 25, 2016; http://www.nytimes.com/2016/02/28/magazine/what-google-learned-from-its-quest-to-build-the-perfect-team.html?_r=0

63 Duncan, *Discovering Phi*. In partnership with the CFA Institute. For more on phi and its use with organization measurement, see Appendix 2.

64 *Ibid.*

65 Daniel Pink, *DRIVE* (New York: Riverhead Books, 2011).

66 Duncan, *Discovering Phi*, p. 20.

67 Ellis, *The Index Revolution*, p. 133.

68 Institutional Investors Senior Delegates Roundtable, Palm Beach, February 17, 2017.

69 Duncan, *Discovering Phi*, p. 17.

70 *Ibid.*, p. 20.

CHAPTER FOUR

New Mindsets Part Two: Spiraling Up to the Future

Maslow's theory suggests that a natural evolution from deficiency needs to growth needs may alter the mindsets of investment professionals, especially as the baby boomers age. The second model – spiral dynamics – suggests that entire countries and/or cultures evolve as changing conditions demand.

Spiral dynamics, developed by Clare Graves, provides insights about the evolution of cultures and, for our purposes, investment cultures.[71] The core of Graves's theory is the idea that human evolution is the product of two forces:

1. The challenges of life (i.e., what we must face in order to survive)
2. Our psychology for decision making (i.e., how we meet the challenges)

These two forces are continually interacting with each other. When survival issues become acute, new worldviews (mindsets) emerge to solve the problems that previous worldviews could not handle.

The evolution of mindsets from our earliest ancestors to modern times is shown in Figure 4.1, which is based on the Graves model. The names of these mindsets are shown in the first column. In brackets is the color classification. Graves chose to give colors to each mindset, so as to project a neutral view for each. (ORANGE may be more evolved than RED, but not "better," in the same sense that high school is more advanced than elementary school but not "better." There is a natural evolution in each case.)

Figure 4.1 Spiral Dynamics Model (SDi)Definition: a model that maps out the major developmental mindsets over the course of human cognitive evolution.

Stages of cultural evolution (personality style)	Key Features	Theme	Key Values	Investment Examples	Maslow Level
Integrator YELLOW	Integral Self: personal freedom to all without harm to others or the physical environment. Limit the excesses of self-interest. Focus on self-expression and systemic approaches.	Live life fully & responsibly, with little fear, and with appreciation for all "previous" mindsets.	Purpose Service Ethics Common Good (High SQ, i.e. Spiritual Intelligence)	Just emerging now. The firm of the future.	Higher Purpose Service Greater Good Relatively Little Fear
Communalist/ clan GREEN	Relational Self: collaborative. Share resources among all. Reach decisions through consensus. Liberate humans from greed and dogma.	Seek peace within, and harmony in community.	Trust and Respect Collaboration Communication Development (High EQ)	Bridgeway, Boston Common, Polen, & ESG firms.	Transformation, moving past prior levels, seeing past "me" to "we".
Rationalist ORANGE	Rational Self: search for success and enhance living through strategy and technology. Seek independence and autonomy. Play to win and enjoy competition.	Act in your own self interest by playing the game to win.	Success Winning Competing Excellence (High IQ)	Hedge funds, many traditional active managers.	Mastery Autonomy
Guardian BLUE	Guardian Self: bring order and stability to all things and control impulsivity through a higher authority. Sacrifice now for later rewards. Laws & discipline builds character.	Life has meaning, direction & purpose with pre-determined outcomes.	Organized Principled Practical Detailed Loyal	Vanguard, traditional bank trust departments.	Connection Belonging Loyalty
Impulsive/ Egocentric RED	Power Self: World is a jungle, full of threats. Proud and defiant. expects attention, demands respect.	Be what you are and do what you want, regardless ...	Power Control	Founder run firms with a strong personality in charge.	Security Safety
Tribal Groups, Hunters and Gatherers					Survival

Commenting on this chart, Barrett writes:

What is noticeable about the evolution of the new world views is that significant acceleration has taken place over the last 150 years since the arrival of the Communitarian World View (i.e. Mindset). This world view had its genesis in the Industrial Revolution, which freed people from the land and leveled the playing field in terms of providing opportunities for people to accumulate wealth. This development, along with the evolution of equity and democratic practices, provided people with an opportunity to meet deficiency needs and the need to focus on their self-interest.[72]

Mindsets are very pragmatic. They stay in place as long as the culture maintains its internal stability. When a critical mass of people within a culture is no longer able to meet their needs, then the mindset is contested. A tipping point is reached and a new mindset replaces the former one. A business example of this shift is the current emphasis on teamwork and flatter organizations, as opposed to the old hierarchies. In the old hierarchies, leaders were assumed to have all the knowledge and they told workers what to do. Now, the world demands much more interaction and idea generation at all levels. Companies that are hierarchical are losing out to more nimble and adaptive companies. Again, survival is the key. And that's why we're introducing this framework – spiral dynamics – to our discussion of the investment world. The old model – traditional active management – is struggling, suggesting the timeliness of a new mindset.

Let's look just a bit more at the concept of mindsets before turning to application of spiral dynamics. Mindsets are distinctly cultural rather than ethnic in origin. Barrett writes:

> The magical world view (i.e. mindset) that initiated tribalism is still found in many parts of Sub-Saharan Africa, and the purposeful world that initiated monarchies and religious states is still prevalent in the Middle East. The more advanced, mostly Western democracies, such as the Scandinavian countries, are mostly operating with a Communitarian mindset [GREEN]. The remaining democracies – countries such as the USA, UK, France, Germany and Italy – are mostly operating from an Achievist mindset [ORANGE].[73]

Understanding these mindsets helps to explain much about world events. The ORANGE USA earnestly tries to convert the rest of the world to democracy, even if the mindset of the other country is completely different. In the investment world, a failure of succession from first generation to second is common. Often the first generation has a classic RED mindset, with a powerful founder in place who rules the roost. When a second generation of younger leaders (often very ORANGE in their mindset) evolves, the result is frequently a confused culture of RED and ORANGE in which the worst qualities of each emerge.

The spiral framework allows us to view the asset management industry in a new light. We are wise to follow Einstein's advice to bring in some new thinking to solve the current problems created by the "old" thinking. Spiral dynamics offers a pair of new lenses.

Here's the big idea behind using spiral dynamics to explain the current problems with the investment world. As a culture, the USA and most of the major financial centers, like London or Hong Kong, are bright ORANGE. If USA culture as a nation is ORANGE – and it is – then the investment world is ORANGE on steroids. This phenomenon largely explains why we said, "The foxes have been watching the henhouse." ORANGE plays to win and loves competition. The role of the "hen watcher" should be taken by people with more of a service mentality.

Let's go into a bit more detail on the ORANGE mindset and its characteristics. For starters, ORANGE mindsets are very self-confident. Beck and Cowan write:

> *Self-confidence intensifies as ORANGE becomes convinced of its correctness. This is a "take-charge kind of guy" and "a woman who knows what she wants and how to get it." Both want it all and want it NOW. [Note: This speaks to short-termism and "Masters of the Universe" overconfidence.]*

> *People in this mindset appear materialistic and acquisitive, but that is because money is life's report card and "nice goods" are tangible evidence of successful ORANGE functioning. The thrill of victory and achievement are the real rewards for ORANGE; life is a game in which the second place is the first among the losers. In most of the world, ORANGE is beginning to bloom, while in the US, the Reagan/Bush years with their Yuppies, S&Ls, conspicuous consumption, and the growing deficits may prove to have been the peak of the ORANGE curve. [Note: Indeed, the next mindset, GREEN, has become more evident in the United States in the past decade.]*

> *People are meant to succeed and become winners. This mindset arises in the person or group seeking to exploit opportunities to create the "good life"; navigating among failures to successes; manipulate events and persons who contribute to the bottom line; employ a vast array of analytical problem-resolution skills for optimized solutions; and orchestrate complex decisions. In addition, ORANGE embraces values and beliefs that stress materialism over spiritualism, pragmatism over principle, and short-range victories over longer term guarantees.*

> *Multiplistic thinking is comparative; life is competitive. The absolute, ideological standards of BLUE are replaced by situationalism and prudent pragmatism – doing what works while saying what they want to hear. [Truly, that is spot on. Think of the rhetoric spoken before the 2008 crash …] Flexibility and rapid responses to a changing marketplace are the "name of the game." However, when naïve ORANGE managers take charge of organizations they try to drive out the old BLUE [i.e., bureaucratic, cautious, process types] through layoffs and forced retirements, producing houses of cards without loyalty to the mission and a pack of competitive underlings out for themselves. [Note: Think Chainsaw Al and Enron.] Little is sacred except growth and expansion. Principles are gelatinous and ethics tend to be overlooked in the rush towards quick prosperity.[74]*

Interestingly, Beck and Cowan wrote these passages in 1996, well before Enron, Bernie Madoff, or the crash of 2008. Their identification of a trend toward unethical behavior proved remarkably accurate.

Having sat through many strategy offsites with investment leaders, we can assure the reader that this mindset accurately characterizes much of what we experience. Again, we are not interested in blaming the ORANGE mindset for all the industry's troubles. The point is simply that this mindset behaves in predictable ways, some of which are very useful in active management and some of which are … less useful. The drive and creativity of investment professionals are admirable, sometimes breathtaking. But the push to win at all costs, fudging ethics, and ignoring client concerns can cause the problems, like low trust, that the industry now faces.

Given the bright ORANGE nature of the investment world, it's no wonder that it attracts personality styles that naturally love problem solving, winning, and competition. In FCG's work with investment firms, we perform various psychometrics, such as Myers-Briggs and the Enneagram. We've collected data over the years showing that the overwhelming Myers-Briggs type in the investment world is the "INTJ" type. In short, INTJ means: introverted, big-picture, thinking, and disciplined types. One leading authority on Meyers-Briggs organizations, William Bridges, describes them this way:

The INTJ Organization

Introverted – takes cues and draws power from within, is fairly closed

Intuitive – concerns itself with possibilities, attends to the big picture

Thinking – depends on impersonal procedures and principles

Judging – likes things spelled out and definite, seeks closure

The INTJ organization is independent, innovative, iconoclastic, and likely to regard itself as unique. Often focused on intellectual or scientific ventures, INTJ organizations are best at developing some essential idea into a service or a product, or else applying an existing idea to some entirely new area. Forceful and undeterred by convention, they make decisions fairly quickly and accurately. They dislike inefficiency and will never settle for something because it has always been done that way.

The INTJ forte is strategy, however, not tactics. Often the creative solution is more interesting to the organization than the detailed plan of turning it into a viable product. [Hence the investment industry's love of sophisticated, complex solutions that often have little utility for the ordinary person.] And there is even a tendency for the organization to want things to conform to the intellectual model rather than accepting things as they are. [Very accurate in light of the "Capital Asset Pricing Model," which is elegant but not based on realistic assumptions.] So the INTJ organization's results sometimes fall short of the expectations people have for them. [Edelman data would support this statement: the investment industry has fallen way short of expectations.]

The INTJ organization has another serious failing. It is likely to be insensitive to the human aspects of whatever it is doing. [Classic ORANGE behavior, as it focuses on tasks and achievements, rather than relationships and emotions.] This may mean that it underestimates the external distress caused by its actions and that employee reactions are unforeseen. The organization is likely to expect employees to subordinate personal concerns and see the logic of the situation. When people react to its actions with strong feeling, it always complains that they are over-reacting. [FCG hears this a lot from investment leadership: dismissing workers' concerns as petty and labeling them "troublemakers."]

The INTJ organization is fairly impervious to criticism. [Self-confidence bordering on arrogance is often found in investment firms.] It is hard for outsiders to get much of an idea about how it functions, which mutes criticism by hiding what is going on. [Especially in the hedge fund industry, which is very secretive.] But it also generates criticism among people who are suspicious of what they cannot see. The self-confidence with which the organization steers its own course can turn into stubbornness, and if the organization gets off on the wrong track somehow, that stubbornness can be disastrous – because INTJ organizations do not easily admit that they have been wrong. They succeed by willpower, and they fail by willpower. [Lots of examples of firms and individuals whose stubbornness got them in trouble. Bill Miller, perhaps? 15 years of outperformance all thrown away in one year by doubling down on financials in 2009.]

They are internally flexible. They expect their employees to be able to shift work groups readily and to handle multiple or ambiguous reporting relationships. They also expect them to understand what is expected of them quickly, and if things must be explained more than once or if a training program does not generate results quickly, there is likely to be impatience. In INTJ organizations, people are supposed to "get the idea" and not need much detailed direction. [Spot on for many FCG clients. Leaders explain the strategy at one Town Hall meeting and are then frustrated when FCG's survey shows that half the firm does not understand the strategy. One CEO in London, after telling us that he did not like consultants and did not like Americans, then told us that investments was a simple business and did not need a strategy. Meanwhile, the entire staff was begging for a well-articulated strategy.]

They are in more trouble, however, with changes that are forced on them. [Which is the current situation: margins falling, alpha shrinking, and trust eroding.] To be able to choose one's challenges is important to them, and INTJ organizations do not take kindly to pressure. When it is the organization's own inner workings that are the problem, the INTJ organization is in even more trouble and can quickly lose momentum and go into a dangerous period of confusion. [We certainly have seen this phenomenon in the industry. The millennials have thrown some leadership teams into a tailspin: "How do we manage these people? They are so entitled and different from us."]

Rational innovation is their strength. They like to deal with information and are impatient with the softer relational side of communication, which they dismiss as touchy-feely or small talk. [True, but as we'll see soon, the GREEN mindset, with its emphasis on emotional intelligence and "we" thinking, is gaining ground.] So, they don't handle their human relations very well, forgetting that people need appreciation and that there is wisdom of the heart as well as of the head. [FCG has coined the term "ADD" for the industry: appreciation deficit disorder. FCG wrote a white paper called Tribes which shows that the two lesser tribes – operations and sales/client facing – feel underappreciated, disrespected, and unempowered.[75]]

Viewing people as essentially elements in a system, they have a rather narrow concept of support and motivation. This can work for highly technical researchers, but it doesn't work so well for other kinds of employees, who often feel that they have been forgotten and taken for granted.

At their best, such companies are very creative: AT & T's Bell Labs are a famous and very successful example. At their worst, they are simply demanding places with very little heart.[76] [FCG worked with one asset manager that fit this description so closely that we finally resigned the account. They went through six of our consultants, until finally the last one standing said "enough" and we were done.]

In FCG's view, this description nicely captures the ORANGE mindset that is the culture of many investment firms. However, there are exceptions. Due to the sheer size and complexity of the industry, some firms are notable exceptions to this ORANGE description.

Vanguard, for example, is decidedly BLUE in its orientation. Jack Bogle has created a cult following for his principled approach to investing in index funds. If you have visited Vanguard in Malvern, it feels decidedly different from many other investment firms. As one leader said to us, "I bleed the company colors." He loves it there, as do his co-workers. There is very much a fundamentalism at Vanguard: "We know the truth and it will set you free!" Apparently, the fervor is spreading, as Charley Ellis titled his new book, *The Index Revolution: Why Investors Should Join it Now*.[77] BLUE is characterized by true believers and Vanguard has a huge following.

There are also a lot of RED investment firms, some very successful. These firms were typically founded by a strong leader – the power figure – who rules with an iron fist. As mentioned earlier, FCG has worked with many of these firms as they struggle with the transition of power from first generation to second. As you can imagine, these are tough assignments because the founder's mindset is RED and it is very unnatural for such people to pass power on to the next generation. This challenge strongly affects sustainability for firms.

What we find very interesting is the emergence of GREEN asset managers. In Chapter 5, we'll look at the catalysts that have moved firms from the ORANGE to the GREEN mindset. For now, here is a description, again from Beck and Cowan, of the GREEN mindset:

> On December 14, 1992, The Wall Street Journal printed an article entitled "Business Books Emphasize the Spiritual." The gist of the piece was that "greed is out." [Note: the investment industry being bright ORANGE was not in the forefront of this shift to GREEN!] It went on to say, "instead of comparing business to war, the operative metaphor in the new business guides is the corporation as family or tribe. Forget intimidation: hip managers are into 'empowerment.'" The Journal is identifying the ORANGE to GREEN transition in the business book market, if not in the business schools. [Note: one of your authors attended University of Chicago in 1979-80, famous for shareholder maximization and efficient market theory. There were no courses in leadership, and no emphasis on teamwork.] Next comes love, acceptance, and spiritual transformations. [And certainly no courses on love, acceptance, or spirituality!]

> Literally thousands of private and public sector organizations are in the throes of ORANGE to GREEN oscillations. From Ben & Jerry's Ice Cream and Apple Computer to the U.S. Army and the Dutch police, issues of lifestyles, organizational responsibility and citizenship, and the company, agency as extended family are occupying key decision makers' time. The bottom line, of necessity, includes much more than dollars; it must make sense once employees become assets to nurture instead of expenses to cut. How people feel about work (and each other AT work) will join the parade right behind the quality and re-engineering bandwagons. Before teams can self-manage, they must first become teams; and that means the "company" cannot become an adversary, nor the "union" a warrior. Both must share common goals on common ground.

> The individual in ORANGE to GREEN is still entrepreneurial, but needs a circle of friends to join the business in a caring [but profitable!] confederation. Many creative start-ups have been initiated in ORANGE/GREEN gatherings of odd ducks, only to

flounder because the ducks refused to include a few ORANGE lone eagles in marketing and some BLUE homing pigeons to keep up with inventory accounts. [Again, the message is that each mindset brings gifts, so skillful leaders will use the talents wisely. More on that later.] At the extremes, interpersonal dynamics become the focus of the organizational "culture" on the assumption that productivity follows harmony.

Yet entering ORANGE/GREEN is still unwilling to commit fully and "let it all hang out." The ORANGE needs for control limit the openness and trust such a culture requires. [Note: FCG has received many requests from investment firms to teach and train teams on the skills of openness and trust.] Risks are to be taken with capital and concepts, not feelings. [Note: Brene Brown, a psychology professor, has rocked the TED talk world recently with a set of videos on "vulnerability." Her point: Creativity and trust will not happen unless team members are vulnerable with one another. As mentioned earlier, Google found that psychological safety was the key factor in the most productive teams.] Instead of complete transparency, we find the jolly-good-fellow who takes pleasure in conviviality and "meaningful" interactions, but keeps a couple of personal options open. [FCG calls this behavior pseudo teamwork. We worked with a senior investment team that was struggling with the new investment environment. In their "come-to-Jesus" session, they asked each senior team member if s/he was "all in." The resounding response was "Yes, we are all in!" The next week, one of the senior team members took a job at a competitor! That is pseudo teamwork: keeping a couple of personal options open!]

You should also beware of the "ORANGE in GREEN clothing" – strong ORANGE or even clever, well-coached RED who knows how to "talk-the-talk" – that is, put on the GREEN façade to get something they want. [With the emergence of ESG, many industry observers argue that investment firms are doing ESG simply to remain relevant, even when they have no real interest in the merits of ESG.][79]

There is strong market evidence that this ORANGE/GREEN combination is very powerful. Later in this book, we'll look at companies that have operated from a true ORANGE/GREEN mindset and have outperformed market averages by significant amounts. But first, let's look at the catalysts that are forcing the change from a predominantly ORANGE mindset to a combination of ORANGE/GREEN and even a YELLOW mindset. After all, the spiral dynamic model is premised on survival. If firms are prospering and all is well, then there would be no need to change. As we saw in Chapter 2, that's not the case: The times they are a-changing.

Summary:

- Spiral dynamics proposes that mindsets evolve over time as conditions warrant.

- The investment industry includes firms that have RED, BLUE, ORANGE, and GREEN mindsets, but the industry is predominantly ORANGE.

- ORANGE mindsets rally around values like success, winning, competition, excellence, and money. Individualist orientation, "I."

- GREEN mindsets are emerging in the investment industry, embracing values like trust, respect, collaboration, and development. Collective orientation, "we."

- Importantly, all these mindsets tend to see their own goals and values as the "right" ones, dismissing the relevance and legitimacy of others. For example, ORANGE has trouble seeing the value of RED, BLUE, or GREEN.

---

[71] Don Edward Beck & Christopher Cowan, *Spiral Dynamics* (Blackwell Publishing, 1996). As mentioned earlier, many other big thinkers have developed their own versions of this model, such as Ken Wilber, Kegan, Barrett, Fowler, and Loevinger, et al.

[72] Barrett, *Well-Being*, p. 293.

[73] *Ibid.*

[74] Beck & Cowan, *Spiral Dynamics.*

[75] See our website for the paper: www.focuscgroup.com

[76] William Bridges, *The Character of Organizations* (Boston: Nicholas Brealey, 2000).

[77] Ellis, *The Index Revolution.*

[78] https://www.ted.com/talks/brene_brown_on_vulnerability

[79] Beck & Cowan, *Spiral Dynamics*, p. 262.

CHAPTER FIVE

The Catalysts: Forces for Change

W e've already touched on the major catalyst: the bottom line. Profit margins are shrinking, with alpha seemingly harder to find and fees under pressure. But there are two other big forces for change that factor into the New Era: millennials entering the workforce and aging baby boomers leading it and leaving it.

Millennials' behavior is explained nicely by our two models, Maslow and spiral dynamics. On the Maslow side, millennials seem genuinely interested in more than just the deficiency needs. They want to meet those needs, as we all do, but they aspire at young ages to the growth needs as well. In terms of spiral dynamics, they seem very open to the GREEN mindset, which embraces values like "larger purpose," "collaboration," and "transparency."

A fair question is, "But, hey, are millennials really that different?" After studying the millennials extensively, Gallup wrote a report on them which opened with its CEO, Jim Clifton, saying that millennials are "profoundly different."

FCG agrees, having seen their impact on investment cultures. In fact, the impact for some firms is so profound that they asked FCG to develop trainings for their managers in how best to lead millennials. Figure 5.1 shows the combined vote from roomfuls of investment leaders on the topic of managing millennials.

Figure 5.1 VOTE: Managing millennials effectively is an important topic.

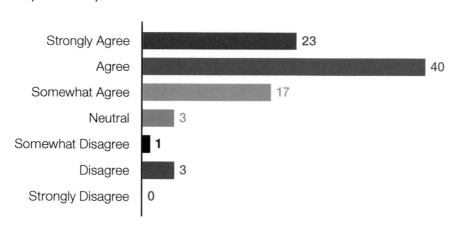

Only four dissenting votes. And these four leaders were not dragging their knuckles and breathing heavily through their mouths – quite the opposite: they were sharp, good leaders. Their rationale for voting no: "If you are a good manager, then you need to understand your people and deal with each of them individually." Each *did* manage millennials and was doing it successfully because they *were* acknowledging the uniqueness of each employee on their team. What these four excellent leaders failed to realize is that many of us could use a heads-up regarding millennials. We don't necessarily see them as different, so we make the mistake, in our busy work days, of treating them like baby boomers or generation Xers: that is, like older workers. Even if we do see the millennial difference, it still doesn't answer the question: "So, are there new rules that work for boomers, Xers, *and* millennials? If so, what are they? And how does a firm implement them? And why should we adjust to them?"

Let's answer the last question first with a few facts. The millennial generation is the largest generation to enter the workforce, at 83 million. Like the baby boomers, the millennials will force us to rethink how we work simply by the sheer force of their numbers in the working population. At this point they already represent more than 50% of the workforce and by 2025 that number will be 75%. Like it or not, the millennials will have a significant impact on how work gets done because they will be doing the work.

It's also useful to understand how each generation has evolved, because the natural friction across generations has an impact on the work environment and our ability to evolve that environment. Much of who we are at work is a product of the key influences that shaped our values. In broad terms, this is a reflection of how we grew up, especially in our adolescence or "wonder years" (ages 11-19). FCG has researched this topic and spoken with hundreds of managers at all levels in investment organizations. Workplace friction is driven by the difference in core values of each generation, the values that influence how they view work, relationships, and communication. These differences drive their expectations of themselves and other generations.

Baby boomers have often been accused of living to work, rather than working to live. Identity comes from their role in an organization, level of success (as defined by promotions and/or compensation; ORANGE), and a desire to be respected as a consequence of both. This is how boomers were trained and influenced. They saw their "builder" predecessors, who lived through the Great Depression and WWII, create a generation of workers founded on loyalty, opportunity, and wealth creation. In the United States, a strong middle class emerged from the ingenuity, sweat, and perseverance of the builders. This further explains how leaders in the investment industry have created an ORANGE environment.

Perhaps boomers were not as loyal as builders (35 years and a gold watch), but they made far fewer job changes than Xers and millennials over the course of their careers. Boomers were the first generation to be more broadly college educated. In the investment industry, boomers have been the founders and leaders of many asset management firms. They value loyalty, hard work (putting in the time), respect, and success (and all the trappings that go with it). Boomers have thrived on economic advances, great investment markets, global economies and, yes, credit (sorry, millennials). These factors have influenced how boomers see themselves and the generations that follow.

Generation Xers were heavily influenced by several major changes in U.S. culture, most notably a substantial increase in the U.S. divorce rate (hence the "live to work" aspect of boomers) and two-parent incomes. This change led to a steep increase in the number of "latchkey" kids (kids who had dual-income or single-parent households and were often by themselves). These two influences formed the Xers' core values of independence and autonomy, the need for balance, and a greater focus on health and well-being. In the investment industry, in particular, the influence Xers have had is more targeted than broad. Much of this is due to the population size of this cohort, which is why FCG's research shows the DNA of the industry to still be more driven by boomer values (ORANGE). However, this is changing, as our data are showing a significant rise in the desired values of leadership development/mentoring, work life balance, and continuous improvement. The millennials are already having an influence.

It is very clear that the previous generations have built the industry based on ORANGE thinking in part because of their heritage and life experience. Based on their own early life experience, millennials have formed some deep core values that will have an influence on the way the industry will work in the future and require a GREEN evolution. Millennial values and experiences have shaped their view of work and life. For example, our leaders in the millennial trainings knew from experience and instinct what the top motivators would be for the younger workers. In the vote graphed in Figure 5.2, you see three clear winners, which line up with FCG's experience and research.

Figure 5.2 VOTE: Top 3 factors in millennial engagement.

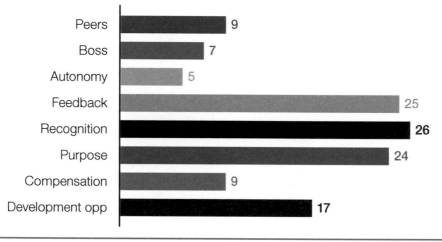

We'll discuss each of these important millennial values – the "Big 6" – in the rest of this chapter:

1. Recognition/appreciation (providing feedback on jobs well done)
2. Feedback/transparency (open communication, lots of feedback, no secrets)
3. Purpose (meaningful work, making a difference, "phi")
4. Development (which includes opportunities to grow and learn)
5. Autonomy (made possible by technology)
6. Causes (charitable contributions, community action)

Recognition/Appreciation

The top vote among leaders was "recognition." Leaders in a work setting tend to use this word and appreciation interchangeably, with both meaning the act of acknowledging good efforts or results. We joked earlier that the investment industry suffers from ADD: appreciation deficit disorder, and it bears repeating. Millennials have grown up as the "trophy generation" where everybody is a winner and everyone gets lots of praise.

Many boomers are put off by what seems like a constant need for attention and praise. To be fair, the business world at large is weak on recognition, with Gallup reporting that "65% of Americans had received no appreciation or recognition in the workplace last year."[80] The simple fact is that all workers want to be recognized for their efforts. Investment leaders do, too. Much of the compensation and rewards work that FCG performs with firms starts with an understanding that there is a lack of recognition. Compensation in the investment industry is a way we keep score and has been applied as a metric for "how much we value a professional." So, even though the conversation may be about money, the underlying desire is to be recognized and validated as a "winner." Research published in Barbara Fredrickson's book *Positivity*,[81] and Kouzes's and Posner's book *Encouraging the Heart*,[82] shows the outward expressions of encouragement:

- boost performance

- strengthen our resolve and resilience

- improve our health

- increase creativity

In addition, recognizing a person:

- gives courage

- inspires

- expands awareness of the value of that person's contribution

- increases self-esteem

- sets their spirits free

Employee recognition affects the bottom line. In their book *The Carrot Principle*, Gostick and Elton demonstrate this.[83] "In response to the question 'My organization recognizes excellence,' the results show that organizations that scored in the lower fourth quartile had an average return on equity (ROE) of 2.4%, whereas those that scored in the top fourth had an average ROE of 8.7%. **In other words, companies that most effectively recognize excellence enjoy a return that is more than triple the return of those that are least effective.**"[84]

Leadership in the New Era must learn that recognition is becoming an even bigger factor in motivating the workforce. Rebecca Fender at CFA Institute makes this point in an article about recognition:

We asked readers whose recognition they valued the most when they accomplish something in their jobs. … Of the 679 respondents, 82% value recognition from others, while only 18% say internal satisfaction is what matters most.[85]

Despite the common view that good work is its own reward, most investment professionals want recognition – and they mostly want it from clients and senior colleagues at their firm. Avoid accepting this truth at your peril.

Feedback/Transparency

Millennials expect feedback and full transparency in the workplace. They are suspicious of "need-to-know" communication policies, and they are quick to see through pseudo transparency. Old-school, command-and-control thinking revolves around the concept that leaders have the information/solutions and workers execute their orders. This approach was in full swing in the 1950s and 60s, when businesses were built on the classic military model from the "greatest generation" who served in WWII. As the workplace shifts from command-and-control to facilitative leadership, where collaboration is the rule, the millennials are asking the obvious question: "Why can't we have full access to information?" The knee-jerk response from many boomer bosses is a chest-grab of fear: "Are you kidding?! We'd lose all control!" (One leader smirked, "You're suggesting we give the keys to the inmates?" Then it was *our* turn to do a chest-grab: *You think of your staff members as inmates?!*)

The point here is to increase the effectiveness of your workforce and meet them where they are, not where *you* are. You may be asking, "Why is transparency such a big deal to millennials?" We are all products of our environment and for millennials the environment has always been instant information (via smartphone, computer, tablet, etc.). They have grown up with the world at their fingertips, so information flow and transparency are natural and normal. For boomers, this has not been the case, simply because they grew up in a need-to-know environment. And there's the rub. The shift is easily explained like this: when boomers were young, where did they get information? Parents, teachers, bosses. And millennials? Instantly, from their phone, laptop, or tablet. No authority figure needed.

To be clear, some information requires confidentiality for legal reasons or for reasons of integrity (a promise made *not* to share information). We understand that, but far too often leaders withhold information just because "we've never shared it before." In other words, there is no valid reason to withhold. It's just the way that ORANGE/BLUE/RED have always done it. FCG has seen many cases of increased trust, respect, and morale when leaders open the kimono and begin to share more information with staff members. As a rule of thumb, Gallup recommends at least one face-to-face meeting with each of your direct reports weekly.[86]

Purpose

Gallup describes this change as "Purpose over Paycheck." A survey of millennials showed the following shocker: More than 60% would rather make $40K in a job they love than $100K in one they think is boring. One of the participants in the classroom mentioned earlier commented, "I tried to influence my millennial daughter to go into investing and she stopped me and said, 'Mom, I'd rather shoot myself. I like working in a rescue shelter.'" Okay then. Boomers and Xers – the older generations – seem to understand this drive for purpose and chose it as a top three motivational factor in the vote described earlier.

We know what you're thinking: They don't care about money right now because they are young and have fewer responsibilities ... just wait! Some of that may be true, but consider a few facts:

1. A core value for millennials is purpose, so as they get older they may want both (money with meaning).

2. Millennials have framed success differently at their core; technology has and will enable them to have better experiences that require less "stuff."

3. Millennials will marry and have children later in life, which means they can focus on the first two points for a longer period.

So, what's to be done to increase engagement and retention of talent *now*?

If you want to engage millennials, you need to understand their desire to do something meaningful – and meaningful does not mean "make a lot of money." (Note: Remember that ORANGE mindsets would believe that making a lot of money is a perfectly good cause!) Investment leaders must be able to articulate why/how their firm is contributing to a better society. In FCG's view, this should be an easy task. The investment function is crucial to happiness, but many older leaders have trouble with articulating their firm's contribution. They've never really thought about it. They are practical people who are deep into running the firm. Purpose doesn't really enter into their thinking. For example, in a speech to nearly 70 sales leaders from major investment firms, FCG asked the leaders if they consider their work to be: A) a job, B) a career, or C) a calling. The response from the group is shown in Figure 5.3.

Figure 5.3 How do most sales professionals in our industry think of their work? It's a

7

54

5

A **Job:** working to complete the task and get paid.

B **Career:** advancement over time, proud of my work, putting in the time it takes to be successful.

C Calling: devotion to my work to serve others, be part of something larger than myself. Money is not the primary driver.

Of course, there is nothing wrong with "jobs" or "careers." We all need to make a living. Nevertheless, given the importance of financial well-being, investments could certainly be elevated to a calling: "a strong feeling that you must do a particular type of job, especially one that you consider morally good."[87] The investment industry is helping people meet a primary need in life. So, as a leader of millennials, be able to articulate a solid reason why the firm contributes to a better world. For example, the earlier suggestion: "Our firm exists to positively influence people's financial well-being."[88] See? It doesn't have to be tricky, just clear and purposeful.

Development

In the graph in Figure 5.2, the fourth highest vote-getter is "development opportunities." FCG sees this factor in all the culture work we do. The biggest gap value in firms – that is, the difference between what firms "have" and what they "want" – is "leadership development/mentoring." (Note: Jim can tell you that in bright ORANGE days, when he started in the industry, this statement was *not* true. None of his young co-workers asked managers for "development and mentoring.") To show you how millennial-dependent this factor is, look at the "want" vote in one firm where we sliced the data by age groups. Employees at the same firm were asked to select 10 values that they want more of. Figure 5.4 shows what the boomers said.

Figure 5.4 Top 10 Values – Aspirational Culture: Baby Boomer

N = 44	Number of Responses	ABC firm Percent
Client Satisfaction	**26**	**59%**
Ethical/Integrity	**25**	**57%**
Collaboration/Teamwork	**25**	**57%**
Excellence/Continuous Improvement	**24**	**55%**
Results Oriented	**20**	**45%**
Professional	**17**	**39%**
Respect	**17**	**39%**
Meritocracy	**17**	**39%**
Balance (Home/Work)	**16**	**36%**
Accountability/Responsibility Long-term Perspective/Vision, Loyalty tied	**12**	**27%**

Green = Match between top existing and aspirational values. Bold values do not appear in the overall Top 10 list of values but are strong in the noted workgroup.

Notice that there is no demand for "leadership development/mentoring." Now look what the same firm's millennials said (Figure 5.5).

Figure 5.5 Top 10 Values – Aspirational Culture: Generation Y

N = 133	Number of Responses	ABC firm Percent
Collaboration/Teamwork	**63**	**47%**
Excellence/Continuous Improvement	**61**	**46%**
Ethical/Integrity	**55**	**41%**
Leadership Development/Mentoring	**51**	**38%**
Balance (Home/Work)	**49**	**37%**
Meritocracy	**47**	**35%**
Client Satisfaction	**46**	**35%**
Professional	**44**	**33%**
Respect	**37**	**28%**
Creativity/Innovation	**37**	**28%**

Green = Match between top existing and aspirational values. Bold values do not appear in the overall Top 10 list of values but are strong in the noted workgroup.

Notice that "leadership development/mentoring" comes out as the fourth highest aspirational value, with nearly 40% of firm's millennials choosing it.

Investment leaders understandably respond to a vote like this with the question: "So, what are the millennials asking for?" They want career paths: *What's next for me? How do I learn new skills and progress?* They want coaching and mentoring: *Who will show me the ropes and take a sincere interest in my development?* They want feedback, and LOTS of it. In other words, they want attention. They had it from their "helicopter" parents and from their teachers, now they want it at work. When millennials quit, the exit interviews often reveal, *"I wasn't getting enough face time with my boss."* So, if you want to keep your talented millennials, you'd better find a way to meet these needs. (Read: more GREEN, less ORANGE!)

Growing up in a world of instant gratification has trained millennials to think about development differently. In our experience, this usually relates to the desire for rapid advancement and rotation in an investment shop. Remember that the millennial generation has grown up on affirmation and instant gratification. Why should it be any different in the workplace? The best strategy we have heard for managing this is to create an environment of "sprints." This applies to both project management (more milestones and opportunities for success/failure) and development.

Our experience tells us that advancement for millennials is framed differently than for other generations. Advancement is less about promotions and more about recognition and learning. Creating an environment where development and appreciation are done with shorter duration and a higher frequency of feedback helps leverage two key millennial values: feedback (positive affirmation) and gratification.

We have seen several investment firms address this very effectively despite having flat structures and fewer "promotions." For example, one firm with a shared analyst pool created a development approach similar to karate belts: white, yellow, green, and so on. As junior analysts acquired and demonstrated more skill, they received recognition, certification, and more complex work. This approach leveraged the values of feedback and gratification while improving the employees' skills and expanding their knowledge.

Autonomy

Another important factor for millennial engagement is autonomy. Millennials have grown up with technology, so they understand that knowledge work can be done anywhere. Their mantra is, "work is something you do, not a place you go."[89] Old-school bosses must reprogram their minds to understand this. FCG has responded to this new reality by partnering with Jody Thompson and Cali Ressler, authors of *Why Work Sucks and*

How to Fix it.[90] Jody and Cali developed the Results-Only Work Environment (ROWE) concept and have implemented it globally for firms. They have helped boomers understand the shift from face time to results-only.

We introduced Jody to two investment firms, each one a top firm as measured by leadership, culture, and performance. Interestingly, one firm embraced ROWE and in fairly short order moved to practices like no vacation policy and no office hours. (In other words, take vacation when you want and spend as much or as little time at the office as you wish. Just make sure you deliver results. As Jody is fond of saying, "No results, no job.") The second firm – much more ORANGE and BLUE in mindset – could not make the mental shift and balked at the program. The first firm's CEO told us recently that productivity in his view has increased. The second firm still struggles with bouts of employee discontent, as workers complain about being treated unfairly in the "flex-time" arrangement that was established. With ROWE there is complete autonomy, so all the grumbling about fair flex time disappears! Here's the catch: Managers in ROWE need to be very clear about roles, tasks, and deliverables. In other words, each party must take responsibility.

Autonomy is a huge leverage point for motivating and retaining millennials. The prevailing view that the millennial generation is lazy and entitled is wrong. This generation will work very hard but values balance and freedom. So, to address this need, think of autonomy as currency in how you reward millennials. Leaders who do will find an unexpected response: loyalty. This example shows the value of moving from a military model to a more facilitative approach to leadership. But remember the catch: Clarity, transparency, and clear direction on deliverables.

Causes

Millennials' interest in causes extends well beyond pledging to United Way. Millennials have logged more volunteer hours in their short lives than the Xers and boomers have combined. Investment firms that allow themselves to be a conduit for volunteer opportunities will attract millennials. Increasingly, FCG's clients have set up foundations to support worthwhile causes. A client example: *The mission of our Foundation is to make a positive impact by actively engaging all employees in identifying and supporting charitable organizations of excellence.* Another client donates 50% of profits to its foundation which actively engages in causes like ending genocide on the planet. Talk to your employees. Find out what they care about. Get involved.

Solutions and Common Ground

Wise leaders will pay attention to the needs of millennials because that cohort will be much of the workforce in the coming years. In short, FCG offers these tips:

1. Accept that millennials bring new values and attitudes (additional GREEN) to the workplace and respond accordingly. The "Big 6" identified earlier are important to millennials and must be addressed in some measure. If you wish to attract and retain top young talent, then you must build a desirable workplace. Millennials differ from prior generations in that they are quick to assess and leave cultures that don't fit their expectations. (Boomers leave jobs after 7 years, Xers after 5, and millennials after 2.)

2. Recognize and leverage the common-ground areas:
    - **Collaboration/teamwork.** As you saw from the culture survey results in Figures 5.4 and 5.5, all generations embrace collaboration. So, you can always bring conflict back to "We all want to work well as a team." Invoke mutual purpose and work out a solution.
    - **Respect/trust.** These pillars of strong culture are also important to both generations. Willingness to understand and respect different viewpoints builds trust. Take a curious stance toward different values. Don't be the leader in the Figure 5.6 cartoon. Remember that each mindset – BLUE, ORANGE, etc. – believes that it has the right way to survive and progress. Boomers often get hung up on the notion: "Hey, that's not the way things were done when I was just starting out." Right. It's not. We're moving from ORANGE to GREEN.

Figure 5.6

Courtesy of WuMo by Mikael Wulff and Anders Morganthaler

— **Accountability.** Each generation accuses the other of being "entitled." Entitlement ends where accountability starts. (And by "accountability" we don't mean "blame," we mean taking responsibility.) FCG has found that all generations embrace accountability. The key is to create accountability while eliminating fear and blame. This shift can be accomplished through clear roles, responsibilities, decision rights, and goals, with the addition of skillful feedback (both positive and negative). FCG has yet to hear talented millennials, Xers, or boomers say, *"No way. We do NOT want that sort of accountability here!"* It is acceptable to all three generations.

Returning to our four dissenting leaders mentioned earlier, we applaud them for doing a fine job managing millennials. Our advice to them? Keep up the good work, but please, don't spread the gospel that "all generations are the same, just be a good manager and you'll do fine." Why? The investment world is changing from ORANGE to GREEN. We all need to understand the new mindset. Many of us are not born leaders and we need all the help we can get. The tips offered in this chapter will help. If you ignore them, you may lose some talented workers – and it won't be like the old days where they "quit and stay." They will quit and leave!

So, in addition to margin pressures, the changing demographics of the workforce will definitely force changes in the industry. Not just in the way millennials are led, but also in the way they invest. As clients of your investment firm, they want to be treated differently. Their GREEN mindsets will expect different conversations with their advisors about finances. They will also want to use technology much more heavily than boomer clients. This is where the importance of the YELLOW mindset comes in. YELLOW is the next evolution up from GREEN. The significance of the YELLOW mindset is that it is the first one that embraces all the previous mindsets. YELLOW does not say, "My way is the best; they must all use my way." Instead, YELLOW leaders will skillfully design marketing and sales initiatives that address the specific needs of the different generations and mindsets. More on that later, but first let's cover the reasons why boomers also represent a powerful force for change.

The Maslow model is key to understanding why boomers will force change. If we think of the millennials as a bottom-up force for change, then boomers represent a top-down force. As boomers have aged and become leaders of investment firms, some have naturally become more curious about the growth needs at the top of the Maslow hierarchy. Most investment leaders have sufficiently mastered their deficiency needs. They certainly have enough money: all of them are members of the 1% club. Most of them have families, club memberships, friends, religious affiliations, and so on. Also, by definition, as investment leaders, they have achieved mastery in their chosen profession. The only thing that keeps them anchored in the deficiency needs is their card-carrying membership in the ORANGE club. One reason we have strong passion for writing this book is to invite these investment leaders to consider awakening from the ORANGE trance. We are thinking now of a long-time friend of ours who has made a fortune in the investment business. (For him, it was truly a business, not so much a profession!) One day, in a moment of openness, we asked him directly why he was – and still is – driven to make so much money. His response was quick and simple: "I don't know, really. I guess once you start making money, it's fun and you just want to keep making it." Spoken like a true addict. (Of course, there is strong evidence now from the neuroscientists that making money can become a chemical addiction, like booze or cocaine.) But it is possible to break the addiction. FCG knows one analyst who left a hedge fund for a 90% pay cut at a long-only firm. The reason: quality of life. The kicker: this analyst received calls and emails from former colleagues congratulating him and asking, "How did you do it?!" They were envious that he had "kicked the habit."

Here's the danger of not meeting your growth needs. Barrett argues convincingly, in his book on the psychology of human well-being, that the growth needs push to be heard. He writes,

> To achieve optimum physical health, we must learn to master each stage of psychological development. We must learn to let go of the ego's fears about meeting our survival, safety and security needs and fully embrace the soul's [Higher Self, mature self] desires for self-expression, connection, and contribution. To test my hypothesis, I first identified the leading causes of death in Western society and then identified the ages when the symptoms of these diseases became prevalent.[91]

Barrett explores each level of the Maslow hierarchy based on the age ranges that are appropriate for achieving the needs. In Barrett's summary of this research, he states,

> What I have attempted to show …, based on data I have gathered from many sources, is that our physiological health is intimately linked to the struggles we have in meeting our ego's needs [i.e., deficiency needs] and our soul's desires [i.e., growth needs].

Barrett's basic point is that our desire to grow as we age is critical to our happiness, or "well-being." This point was introduced earlier in the quote from Duncan: "Consequently, 84% of all investment professionals report being demotivated in some way, and 68% reported having medical issues as a result of stress."[92]

If we're not satisfying our needs – deficiency or growth – then we suffer. This makes intuitive sense. The happiest people we know are indeed living from the higher aspirations of making a difference and being of service. Hence, the invitation to investment leaders is to get curious about your own growth. Have you moved beyond the lure of the ORANGE mindset – to be wealthy, successful, and powerful – and embraced your soul's desire to connect, create, and contribute?

Let's summarize where we've been and where we're going. The big reframe in this book is moving from abstract concepts like benchmarks, alpha, and efficient frontiers to simple happiness for all the people involved: investment professionals, clients, shareholders, employees, and other stakeholders, like the community. By losing sight of the real goal – happiness – the deeply ORANGE investment community has put their excellent minds to use designing products and innovations that often are not useful and, at worst, are harmful. (Remember Volcker's ATM comment.) We reviewed the industry fundamentals, which are deteriorating, and measures of success, like the Edelman Trust Barometer, which showed the lowest industry score except for media. To better understand why this happened and discover a way out, we introduced two models that provide new frameworks, à la Einstein and the need for new thinking. Maslow's hierarchy of needs describes a path to more happiness via meeting the growth needs: moving from "me" to "we." Graves's spiral dynamics idea describes mindsets that drive behavior. Finally, we explored three big catalysts for change. First, and most obvious, is the crisis in the industry fundamentals, or as McKinsey puts it, "a once-in-a-generation shift in competitive dynamics."[93] Second is the huge inflow of millennials into the workforce, with their different mindsets concerning money, purpose, and happiness. Third is the aging of the baby boomers, which naturally positions them to care more about Maslow's growth needs.

With the stage set, let's move on to explore the key mindsets and how they appear to be shifting.

Summary:

- Profitability and survival are powerful change factors. Most asset managers are facing those issues now.

- Demographics is another big catalyst for change: millennials and baby boomers.

- Millennials are much more motivated by Maslow's growth needs, especially purpose, than are earlier generations.

- Millennials are also motivated by appreciation, transparency, development/training, autonomy, and social causes.

- Baby boomers have met many of their deficiency needs and are naturally positioned to aspire to the growth needs of purpose, greater good, and service.

- Research indicates that ignoring the growth needs can lead to emotional and physical problems later in life.

---

80 Judith Mills & Joan Shafer, "Employee Recognition: A Lynchpin Value for Cultural Transformation" (September 2010), p. 1; http://www.nine-dots.org/documents/Employee%20Recognition%20 in%20the%20spotlight.pdf

81 Barbara Fredrickson, *Positivity* (New York: Random House, 2009).

82 James Kouzes & Barry Posner, *Encouraging the Heart* (San Francisco, CA: Jossey-Bass, 2003).

83 Adrian Gostick & Chester Elton, *The Carrot Principle* (New York: Free Press, 2009).

84 Mills & Shafer, "Employee Recognition," p. 6.

85 Rebecca Fender, "The Words We Long to Hear: Well Done!," *Enterprising Investor* (December 16, 2016); https://blogs.cfainstitute.org/investor/2016/12/16/the-words-we-long-to-hear-well-done/?s_cid=eml_Selections&mkt_tok=eyJpIjoiTmpneE16ZGhZbUk0WVRKbSIsInQi OiJzQzdwOWtrWk5TNDd6MU9mTlpMM0xRS05LNlFmUHpkbGZQa2hvbUc5T3RxVUtjWFFIa2 ZYWU00ZHFrcGQwTHRDXC9NdVJPcEYrdWwzMHpsMU8zWlpRd0pWaIJOdktoOEY1QX MyeUEyTVhBdDZpV3FVY1R5MVlER0NWQIA0czNnMXYifQ%3D%3D

86 \<Gallup recommendation source.\>

87 http://www.macmillandictionary.com/dictionary/british/calling

88 Thanks to Michael Falk on our team, as he first suggested this purpose statement which was the driving force behind his book on entitlements and sustainable economic growth. See his website for more on the book and how to order a copy: www.letsalllearnhowtofish.com

89 Thanks to our strategic partner Jody Thompson for this quote and many insights about autonomy.

90 Jody Thompson & Cali Ressler, *Why Work Sucks and How to Fix It* (New York: Penguin Group, 2010). For more on results-only work environments, see www.gorowe.com

91 Barrett, *Well-Being*, p. 203.

92 Duncan, *Discovering Phi.*

93 McKinsey report, "Thriving in the New Abnormal – North American Asset Management" (November 2016); http://www.mckinsey.com/industries/financial-services/our-insights/ thriving-in-the-new-abnormal-north-american-asset-management

CHAPTER SIX

The Mindsets: Moving from ORANGE to ORANGE and GREEN with YELLOW

R emember that each of the mindsets is useful. They were appropriate for survival at different points of evolution. ORANGE allowed us to move out of the agrarian age into the industrial age. GREEN is emerging as we move fully into the information age. Avoid the trap of deciding that one is better than the rest: They each play a part by building on the former. The guiding principle of spiral dynamics is "transcend and include." As GREEN emerges, the point is not to eliminate all traces of ORANGE – far from it. The investment world was built on ORANGE and needs those skillsets. However, GREEN is also needed to unite passion and purpose in the industry. Think of ORANGE as strong IQ (intelligence quotient), and GREEN as high EQ (emotional intelligence).

Because the ORANGE and GREEN mindsets are central to our new vision, let's lay them out in a table showing the fundamental differences (Table 6.1).[94]

Table 6.1

ORANGE MINDSET (Strong IQ)	GREEN MINDSET (Strong EQ)
Competitive, play to win	Collaborative, play together
Individualist, "me"	Collective, "we"
Assertive, take charge	Receptive, blend in
Rational, logical	Emotional, intuitive
Win/lose	Win/win
Pragmatic	Idealistic
Disciplined, orderly	Flexible, adaptive
Wall Street	Nordic countries
Purpose of business: maximize shareholder value	Purpose of business: maximize all stakeholders' well-being
Lead from the "head"	Lead from the "heart"

Our vision suggests that success in the New Era depends on appreciating the strengths of each mindset and positioning them where they can truly serve. Simply put, ORANGE is perfectly designed for price discovery and competing for alpha. GREEN is brilliantly suited for collaborating with clients and serving. The strength of the YELLOW mindset, which we discuss later, is understanding these differences, appreciating what each mindset contributes, then leveraging the strengths. So, as some firms evolve into a GREEN mindset, they must be careful about not excluding all the value found in ORANGE. In this sense, the approach is like Ken Blanchard's "situational leadership" in which he explored different styles of leadership for different situations.[95] The investment industry has been dominated by ORANGE. For a while that worked and was extremely profitable. But, as with any strength, if overused it becomes a weakness. The overdone ORANGE becomes the Gordon Gekko, Bernie Madoff, subprime debacles which have damaged trust in the industry.

There has always been a bit of GREEN mindset in the investment world; the claim here is not that it is brand new. Rather, it is becoming more common. For example, *Pensions & Investments (P&I)*, a mainstream trade magazine in the investment industry, only started doing a "Best Places to Work" issue in 2012. The investment industry has been around for decades, but is only now focusing on this aspect of work. By contrast, *Fortune* magazine has been running its "100 Best Companies to Work For" for 20 years. The *P&I* issue on "Best Places to Work" is testimony to the onset of GREEN. The first issue of *P&I* Best Places featured 15 winners. The 2016 issue featured 30 winners and listed numerous "additional winners." The 2016 issue also featured sidebars on topics like, "Firms go green to aid environment and themselves at the same time" and "Training, development found as common attributes for winners."[96] Nearly all the write-ups on the winners include GREEN characteristics:

- "Employees' personal lives are valued above work lives, meaning the firm is very flexible, understanding, and accommodating to employees' personal needs."

- "takes care of its employees"

- "creates a positive team environment"

- "promotes a highly intellectually stimulating environment"

- "employees can thrive professionally"

- "important for employees to feel that their organization cares about things outside the business"

- "mission statement: Investing to improve lives"

- "my co-workers are, generally speaking, good people who care about doing the right thing. And there is a legitimate 'client first' culture that makes me proud to be associated with the broader organization"

Again, the descriptions of these firms is a testimony to the rise of GREEN. In FCG's view, the mindset shifts from ORANGE to GREEN can be summarized as in Table 6.2.

Table 6.2

Investment ORANGE	Investment GREEN
Purpose is to win by offering superior investment returns and excellent client service.	Purpose is to genuinely add value for the client and improve people's lives. Often extend the purpose to all stakeholders.
Competitive stars: Peter Lynch, Bill Miller, Bill Gross, and their like.	Collaborative teams, with multiple portfolio managers.
Zero-sum (win/lose): we win for our clients, while other firms lose. Some firms will beat the benchmark, while others won't.	Abundance (win/win): markets rise over time, lifting all "boats." Outcomes for clients are customized, not judged against a benchmark.
Investment alpha: industry's resources go to creating alpha in portfolios.	Household alpha: financial literacy, tax and estate strategies, financial planning and advice.
Value investing: finding mispriced stocks, buying winners.	"Values" investing: aligning investments with client's personal values: ESG, Impact investing, or highest return possible.
Short term: quarterly earnings, yearly performance results	Long term: investing across cycles with long-term goals
Process: the philosophy, discipline, and process are paramount	People: the relationships of trust and respect are paramount
Growth and expansion: grow the client base and assets under management (AUM)	Value add: provide a truly valuable service that makes clients happy, secure, peaceful
Profit driven: our job is to make money in the markets in any legal fashion we can	Societal driven: our job is to help make the world a better place through responsible investing

For those of us who've been in the investment industry for multiple decades, the changes listed here are fascinating. Mindsets have shifted, just as the spiral dynamic advocates would have predicted. At FCG, it has been interesting to work with investment firms that are experiencing this shift from "less ORANGE" to "more GREEN" and to work with their leaders to make the transition. We've had to develop an objective view of each mindset so that we didn't "choose sides." Within our own team, we have members who are more ORANGE and those who are more GREEN. For example, we were on a phone call with a CEO whose firm had just lost a major client. One FCG colleague was more ORANGE, the other GREENer. We listened for a while and then the ORANGE colleague began to discuss strategies for recovering from the loss, structuring the investment teams differently, possibly hiring a few new team members, messaging the loss to the stakeholders and the public, and so on. What became evident to the GREEN colleague was that the CEO was not done expressing her feelings about the loss. This was a long-time client and she was very upset about losing them. GREEN intervened and said, "Tell us a little more about the client and your history with them." She was only too glad to express her feelings of hurt, betrayal, discouragement, and anger. Eventually, when she had gotten that charge off her chest, she returned to the business at hand: what to do now. But this scenario is very characteristic of the ORANGE versus GREEN difference: ORANGEs are thinkers first, feelers second; GREENs are the reverse. The ORANGE colleague went right for the thinking piece: let's strategize about how to recover from this loss. Eventually, this client calmed down – with GREEN's help – and then ORANGE provided excellent advice about how to move forward. Collaboration, emphasizing the respective strengths, is better than trying to work with either strength alone.

As ORANGE and GREEN work side by side, there will be friction. It will be helpful for investment leaders to understand the next mindset in the spiral, YELLOW. This newly emerging mindset is differentiated from ORANGE and GREEN in two key ways:

- YELLOW can see the merits of each previous mindset. The other mindsets, up to this point, can only see the value of their own. ORANGE rationalists think that it is irresponsible for firms to do anything other than make a profit, whereas GREEN mindsets, like Ralph Nader, believe that ORANGE is dangerous, "the root of all evil." YELLOW balances the two, seeing the value of each.

- YELLOW is the first mindset that doesn't operate from fear. As discussed in the Maslow model, when people ascend the needs hierarchy successfully, they become more growth minded, not deficiency minded. They are pulled toward positive, larger goals, rather than driven by the fear and greed of markets.

Hence, one of the big invitations for leaders is to work on becoming more YELLOW in their mindset. How? Already, we are seeing many movements in this direction. For example, one useful practice for becoming YELLOW is meditation, or, to use a more general term, *mindfulness*. The CFA Institute – trade association for the industry – has a staff member Jason Voss, CFA, who was a portfolio manager but is now the Institute's internal expert on meditation and mindfulness. He has written books on the subject and authored many articles published in the CFA magazine. At FCG, we have our own mindfulness expert, Robert Chender. Robert is a lawyer by training, and has served as COO at various investment firms. He has been a trainer in mindfulness for many years, and has been certified by the experts who designed the mindfulness courses for Google and other firms. A side note: Ray Dalio, who founded Bridgewater, arguably one of the most successful hedge funds, claims that meditation has been fundamental to his success.

Spiral dynamics experts explain the need for the YELLOW mindset as follows:

The brightening of every new mindset is a major step in human development. But the GREEN to YELLOW transition is, as Graves called it, "a momentous leap" which takes us over from the First Tier's Subsistence Levels [deficiency] to the Second Tier's Being levels [growth].[97] *This is not just another step along the developmental staircase.*

YELLOW introduces complexity beyond even the best First Tier thinking. Mega-organizations and mega-population masses exist because the subsistence problems are understood, if not fully under control. That introduces mega-problems that make these New Times which definitely call for New Thinking.[98]

Indeed, that is a major premise of this book: Einstein is right in saying that we can't solve the new problems with old thinking. The investment industry will need new thinking to solve its new problems. ORANGE and GREEN will not be sufficient; there will have to be YELLOW leaders who can navigate these complex waters.

The YELLOW mindset defines its qualities as "being independent within reason, knowledgeable so much as possible, and caring, so much as realistic."[99]

While it's unlikely that any one individual will exhibit all the following traits, when YELLOW is emerging as the dominant mindset, a person/group:

- are disciplined not to spend much energy on perfunctory niceties unless they are important to others present [in FCG's terminology, *appropriate candor*]

- will not waste time on interpersonal gamesmanship or pointless interpretations or contrived layers of meaning or semantic trivia [eliminate politics and manipulating]

- value good content, clean information, open channels for finding out more on their own terms, and an attitude of open questioning and discovery [*humble and curious*, in FCG's lingo]

- favor appropriate technology, minimal consumption, and a deliberate effort to avoid waste and clutter [efficient and minimalist in their approach]

- have no need for status, exhibitionism, or displays of power unless a power is demanded by life conditions [eliminate corner offices, company jets, fancy headquarters, except where merited]

- enjoy human appetites but do not become compulsive slaves to any of them [understand that money, like booze and cocaine, can become addictive and manages their appetites]

- are concerned with the long run of time rather than their own life span or those of other humans [invest for the long term, avoids short-termism]

- see life as an up-and-down journey from problem to solution, so both chaos and order are accepted as normal [maintains calm in bull and bear markets]

- replace anything artificial or contrived with spontaneity, simplicity, and ethics that "make sense" [see through regulations to the core need and create a culture to maintain ethics]

- seek after a variety of interests and will elect to do what they like whether or not it is trendy, popular, or valued by others [does not follow the herd]

- cannot be coerced, bribed, or intimidated, as there is no compulsion to control or desire to be controlled by others [has moved up the Maslow hierarchy to the point where they have true integrity]

- will run the gamut of being gentle or ruthless, a conformist or nonconformist, based on the factors involved in a circumstance and the overall interests of life itself [practice situational leadership]

- locate their motivational and evaluative systems within themselves, thus becoming relatively immune to external pressure or judgment [master the three big fears: loss of security, approval, and control. Can be courageous]

People observing the YELLOW leaders may find them strange. RED would certainly find them odd, but perhaps fun to hang out with. BLUE's principled, rather rigid and process-driven mindset might experience them as inconsistent, disrespectful, and out-of-focus. ORANGE sees them as unwilling to commit themselves fully to achieving goals, needing a bit more ambition. From the GREEN standpoint, YELLOW seems cool, reserved, and intellectualizing of emotions without joining wholeheartedly into the group experience.

A key strength of YELLOW is reduced fear, which gives them very clear thinking and vision. They are not thrown by the triggers that affect the previous mindsets. Sometimes when reading about the YELLOW mindset, we think of Collins's

Level 5 leaders[100]: very focused but very ego-less. In fact, that's a good way to think about YELLOW: operating from the Higher Self rather than the Ego. They have highly developed intuitive gifts which allow them to absorb and process a lot of data and then cut to the core of the problem. When analyzing the best investment teams, FCG found that this was a characteristic of the best teams: the ability to see the critical catalysts that drive investment outcomes.

The unique skillsets of YELLOW are:

1. YELLOW is able to move in and out of various mindsets in order to make them functional and show them how to connect and work with other mindsets.

2. YELLOW problem-solvers are adept at resolving paradoxes. They can frame an issue in such a way as to show the dilemma, then show how a "both-and" solution is superior to a forced "either-or" solution. For example, they can find ways to combine the ORANGE's drive for growth and progress with the GREEN concern about the "needs of the people." YELLOW looks beyond win/win, which can still create a third loser, to the ultimate win/win/win. (In Chapter 7, we'll take a closer look at a YELLOW-like leader, John Mackey at Whole Foods, and see how he strives to combine the strengths of capitalism with the strengths of empowering and caring for workers.)

The importance of introducing the YELLOW mindset is that most of us – having been raised in RED, BLUE, ORANGE, or GREEN – hardly notice it, unless we are looking for it. As noted earlier, it just looks different or strange in many respects and so we dismiss it. Many books about leadership are written from the viewpoints of former mindsets.

- RED: Donald Trump writes about *Think Big and Kick Ass* (doesn't that say it all)

- BLUE: Jack Bogle crusades for *Character Counts* and *Saving Capitalism from Short Termism*

- ORANGE: Jack Welch writes on *Winning* (again, classic title for an ORANGE)

- GREEN: James Autry writes on *Love and Profit* ("Make love not war")

In Chapter 7, we will look at John Mackey's book *Conscious Capitalism*, which describes many of the YELLOW mindset qualities. Having explored the YELLOW mindset more fully, we'll then look at investment firms and their leaders that are emerging as YELLOW firms.

Summary:

- ORANGE and GREEN are characterized as the "rationalist" and the "idealist".

- ORANGE tends to be strong IQ, GREEN high EQ (emotional intelligence).

- In the New Era, each mindset will be needed.

- YELLOW is starting to emerge as the mindset that values both ORANGE and GREEN and operates at the top of the Maslow hierarchy, with little fear and a desire to meet the growth needs.

- In YELLOW, the Higher Self has taken charge, with the Ego in service to the Higher Self.

---

[94] For Myers-Briggs fans, these two mindsets look very much like "NTJ" vs. "NFP." The GREEN mindset is very much an "NFP" mindset, or what David Keirsey called the Rationalist and the Idealist temperament. David Keirsey, in *Please Understand Me II* (Delmar, CA: Prometheus Nemesis, 1998) describes the two as follows:

> Rationals are abstract and objective. Seeking mastery and self-control, they are concerned with their own knowledge and competence. Their greatest strength is strategy. They excel in any kind of logical investigation such as engineering, conceptualizing, theorizing, and coordinating.

> Idealists are abstract and compassionate. Seeking meaning and significance, they are concerned with personal growth and finding their own unique identity. Their greatest strength is *diplomacy*. They excel at clarifying, individualizing, unifying, and inspiring.

[95] Kenneth Blanchard & Spencer Johnson, *The One Minute Manager* (New York: William Morrow, 2003).

[96] *Pensions&Investments*, "Best Places to Work in Money Management 2016" (December 12, 2016), p. 22; http://www.pionline.com/specialreports/best-places-to-work/20161212

[97] The reference here is to the same jump in the Maslow model, from deficiency to growth needs.

[98] Beck & Cowan, *Spiral Dynamics*, p. 274.

[99] *Ibid.*, p. 275.

[100] Jim Collins, *Good to Great* (New York: HarperCollins, 2001), p. 17.

CHAPTER SEVEN

YELLOW Leadership: An Example

A ccording to spiral dynamics, YELLOW is just emerging as a mindset. Another way to think of YELLOW is a "conscious" leader. By that we mean that the Higher Self – wisdom and compassion – is guiding the individual, not the Ego. Some refer to this mindset as spiritual intelligence (SQ). Conscious leadership is bringing one's whole self and with total awareness.[101] Clear examples are rare, but arguably these leaders would be candidates:

- Political: Nelson Mandela, the Dalai Lama, Gandhi, Abraham Lincoln

- Spiritual: Martin Luther King, Jr., Mother (Saint) Teresa, Eckhart Tolle

- Sports: John Wooden, Phil Jackson, Joe Maddon (Chicago Cubs, we couldn't resist …)

- Business: John Mackey, Robert Greenleaf, Collins "Level 5 leaders," Allan Mullaly, Ed Catmull

- Scientific: Albert Einstein, David Bohm, Stephen Hawking

- Academia: Peter Senge, Ken Wilbur, Clayton Christensen, Ken Blanchard, John Maxwell

Some characteristics of conscious leaders (YELLOW) were introduced in Chapter 6. Additionally, conscious leaders:

- Are self-aware and introspective. They know who they are and they have a wisdom that is a deeper intelligence, an inner authority.

- Serve from a higher purpose and inspire a vision. They transcend Ego for the greater good of the organization and humanity.

- Have a genuine curiosity to understand others and create a deeper connection.

- Create cultures where others can flourish, feel empowered, and realize their potential.

- Lead with an emphasis on what the "Whole" – employees, customers, stakeholders, and the organization – needs. Connecting with the Whole and aligning purposes creates win/win/wins, sustained results, and better futures.

- Are confident, compassionate, courageous, and can make tough decisions while taking full responsibility for their decisions.

- Practice humility and authentic power. This is power from within rather than a focus on external power based on the trappings of titles and prestige.

- Live life from a place of integrity and wholeness. They are grounded in values, family, community and work.[102]

We don't mean to present John Mackey as the consummate, be-all-and-end-all of business leadership. But in reading *Conscious Capitalism* one finds a host of YELLOW-like approaches and decisions which certainly suggest that he is operating with some YELLOW in his leadership. For example, Mackey opens the book with pure admiration for capitalism and ORANGE. After he abandoned his youthful idealism about social democratic philosophy, he read – "devoured" – dozens of business books. He writes:

> *I learned that voluntary exchange for mutual benefit has led to unprecedented prosperity for humanity … the progress that human beings have collectively made during the past two hundred years is simply incredible. I learned that free enterprise, when combined with property rights, innovations, the rule of law, and constitutionally limited democratic government, results in societies that maximize societal prosperity and establish conditions that promote human happiness and well-being – not just for the rich, but the larger-society, including the poor.[103]*

Note that Mackey ties economic progress and prosperity back to "human happiness and well-being," which is a premise of our book. The investment industry must stay focused on real outcomes, not abstract concepts.

Mackey goes on to cite statistics about the positive impact of capitalism:[104]

- Just 200 years ago, 85% of the world's population lived in extreme poverty (defined as less than $1 a day); that number is now only about 16%. Free-enterprise capitalism has created prosperity not just for a few, but for billions of people everywhere.

- Average income per capita globally has increased 1,000% since 1800.

- In just the past 40 years, the percentage of undernourished people in the world has dropped from 26% to 13%. If current trends continue, we should see hunger virtually eliminated in the 21st century.

- From a world of almost complete illiteracy, we have transformed, in only a couple of hundred years, into one in which 84% of adults can now read.

- Contrary to popular belief, prosperous countries have a higher level of life satisfaction. The self-determination associated with free markets, along with greater prosperity, leads to greater happiness. The top quartile of economically free countries has a life satisfaction index of 7.5 out of 10, compared with 4.7 for the bottom quartile.

Again, Mackey brings his point back to happiness. We keep hammering on this nail because it helps explain our industry's trust problem. Consumers are skeptical because we don't give proper attention to the simple outcome of happiness. That's what people want. Our industry needs to ask itself, "How do we help provide that?" In our view, financial well-being – our deliverable – ranks right up there with the two biggies: health and relationships. Financial advisors hold a hugely influential position in their clients' lives. It's hard to be happy if you are sick, lonely, or broke.[105] We may be able to help with the "broke" piece – and the broke piece ties directly to the sick piece. (Wealth and health are interdependent.)

So, what is the problem facing capitalism? If it has contributed mightily to the happiness and well-being of billions of people, why does it need to change? Mackey identifies four reasons why capitalism is under attack:[106]

1. "Businesspeople have allowed the ethical basis of free-enterprise capitalism to be hijacked intellectually by economists and critics who have foisted on it a narrow, self-serving, and inaccurate identity devoid of its inherent ethical justification. Capitalism needs both a new narrative and a new ethical foundation, one that accurately reflects its intrinsic goodness and virtue. [Based on our new understanding of ORANGE, we can see that Mackey is basically saying that runaway ORANGE has damaged capitalism.]

2. Too many businesses have operated with a low level of consciousness about their true purpose and overall impact on the world. [Maslow would argue that too many business leaders are operating from deficiency needs, not the higher growth needs] Their tendency to think in terms of tradeoffs has led to many unintended, harmful consequences for people, society, and the planet, resulting in an understandable backlash. [Low scores on the Edelman Trust Barometer.]

3. In recent years, the myth that business is and must be about maximization of profits has taken root in academia as well as among business leaders. This has robbed most businesses of the ability to engage and connect with people at their deepest levels. [FCG's experience with millennials has shown this to be true.

Many younger workers are insisting that their firms stand for more than profit. They want to feel that their work is making the world a better place. ESG investors are taking a similar stand.]

4. Regulations and the size and scope of government have greatly expanded, creating the conditions for the spread of crony capitalism, restricting competition in favor of politically well-connected businesses. Crony capitalism is not capitalism at all, but is seen as such by many because it involves businesspeople. [Especially after the crash in 2008, many consumers recoiled from investing because they saw Wall Street and markets as rigged by the big players.]

Mackey summarizes his solution by saying that "the pie grows, and there is more for everyone. This idea is at the core of capitalism's extraordinary and unique ability to generate wealth."[107] Likewise, that is the core of the investment industry's solution: harness the upward trend of markets and financial savvy, so that all benefit. Currently the investment industry operates more with a "casino" mentality: There are a few lucky winners (who chose the right asset managers), lots of losers, and a house that always wins (the investment firms). In the future, the model should shift to leveraging upwardly rising markets in which all can win if they are willing to work and save money. Ellis expresses this same view simply in The Index Revolution: "Everyone can win."[108] This view is radically different from the zero-sum mindset of ORANGE.

Mackey speaks to the heart of the millennial generation – or people of any generation, if they move up the Maslow hierarchy – when he states his vision for a better future:

Business is good because it creates value, it is ethical because it is based on voluntary exchange, it is noble because it can elevate our existence, and it is heroic because it lifts people out of poverty and creates prosperity. Free-enterprise capitalism is one of the most powerful ideas we humans have ever had. But we can aspire to even more. Let us not be afraid to climb higher.[109]

This clear, inspiring vision is lacking at so many investment firms. Instead FCG hears vision statements like:

"We aspire to deliver superior performance over our benchmark."

We work in an industry that has vast potential for improving people's lives by giving them peace of mind around their financial lives. In typical markets, a person might expect to double their savings in less than a decade, without fancy investing. How? Just by buying and holding an index fund!

Mackey gives a nod to the power of the Maslow model when he writes:

"The 'psychological center of gravity' for the U.S. has shifted as a whole into midlife and beyond. This silent passage marked a gradual but significant transformation of the zeitgeist toward midlife values such as caring and compassion, a greater desire for meaning and purpose, and concern for one's community and legacy. Even young people started to exhibit these characteristics; by many accounts, the millennials are the most socially and environmentally conscious generation we have ever seen."[110]

Remember our change argument: the crisis in the investment industry will force change. And two big catalysts will be aging baby boomers and millennials, as they exhibit the values just described.

So, what are the clues that suggest Mackey is working from a YELLOW-like mindset? Consider this passage where he states explicitly that the prior mindsets – which we've covered in earlier chapters – are inadequate to solve today's problems. Again, tirelessly pounding on Einstein's quote about the need for new thinking:

Unfortunately, most companies have not evolved to keep pace with all the changes and are still doing business using mindsets and practices that were appropriate for a very different world. It is now time to change that.[111]

Remember that a characteristic of YELLOWs is that they have moved beyond the deficiency needs that stir up fear. Instead, they are motivated by the Higher Self. Here is Mackey's vision of how businesses in the future should be run:

Picture a business built on love and care, rather than stress and fear. [Remember, 68% of investment professionals indicated high levels of stress.[112]] The team members are passionate and committed to their work. Their days race by in a blur of focused intensity, collaboration, and camaraderie. Far from becoming depleted and burned out, they find themselves at the end of each day newly inspired and freshly committed to what brought them to the business in the first place – the opportunity to be part of something larger than themselves, to make a difference, to craft a purposeful life while earning a living.

Think of a business that cares profoundly about the well-being of its customers, seeing them not as consumers but as flesh-and-blood human beings whom it is their privilege to serve. It would no more mislead, mistreat, or ignore its customers than any thoughtful person would exploit loved ones at home. Its team members experience the joy of service, of enriching the lives of others.[113]

If Mackey sounds a bit too idealistic here, we can assure you that our best clients align with this description. Just ask Fred Martin, whom we quoted earlier in the book. He will tell you that his proudest moments are when he receives handwritten letters from clients, thanking him for the expert advice he's given them over decades. Fred and his colleagues care deeply about "enriching the lives of others" – so much so that they made it into their mission statement: "Enriching lives through long term investing."[114]

Or walk into the break room of Polen Capital in Boca Raton and look at the photos of their clients on the walls. Polen invites teachers, policemen, firefighters, and others to come meet and speak to their staff members. Polen doesn't exist to beat benchmarks, but rather to help real people. Texas Teachers is yet another example. We've asked their investment staff members, "Why don't you go work on Wall Street? You could triple your salary." Their response? "We want to help the teachers who educated our children." This is powerful stuff and lives up to Mackey's noble vision.

Unfortunately, FCG has also sat in numerous strategy sessions that tell the opposite story. Clients are never mentioned. This trend became so pronounced that we are now considering a new practice in strategy sessions: We introduce an empty chair which represents the client's interest. We ask each strategy participant to imagine a real client in that chair and keep them in mind for the entire session.

The worst case that we've encountered occurred during a compensation discussion, when one of the firms' partners uttered the astonishing statement: "We're talking about the partners in this discussion, we don't care about the clients." One of our FCG colleagues, to his credit, challenged the partner. The upshot? That FCG partner who challenged was placed in the "penalty box" and eventually fired from the engagement. In our work, we see the good, the bad, and the ugly … and that was ugly. To use our new language, that was ORANGE at its worst: all Ego, no Higher Self.

What are the core values of a YELLOW mindset organization? Well, in Mackey's Whole Foods, they rally around these values:

• Highest quality products

• Delighting clients

• Happy workers

• Striving for excellence

• Financial security

• Supporting the community and environment

• Looking for win/win/wins

• Teaching health to customers

Notice the last value: teaching the public to be smarter about their food consumption and health. There is a strong parallel here with the investment world: teaching the public to be financially literate. This is an area where investment firms could do a world of good, but precious few are committed to this end. Ariel Investments in Chicago is one of them. Mellody Hobson is passionate about her goal of helping African American families achieve financial literacy.[115] To be fair, there are other firms as well, such as Vanguard, Voya, and SSgA, to name just a few. But the point here is that all investment firms could contribute to this societal benefit. Larry Fink, CEO of the largest asset management firm (Blackrock) stated clearly, "Asset managers also have an important role in building financial literacy, but as an industry we have done a poor job to date … . Now is the time to empower savers with new technologies and the education they need to make smart financial decisions."[116]

Years ago, when Jim was a portfolio manager at Allstate, one of his ancillary jobs was to help design their 401(K) program and then explain it to the regional office employees. They were so grateful to have the most basic financial concepts explained to them in simple terms. Long-time employees would shove their 401(K) statements in Jim's face and beg him for advice. (Of course, he could not legally give them investment advice. But we can tell you that a relatively young Allstate workforce had 60% of its retirement savings in cash – and we all know that wasn't a good idea in the 90s.)

Mackey cites the mission statement of Medtronic as a good example of a compelling and far-reaching vision: "The story of Medtronic is one of men and women who have dedicated their lives and careers to helping real people overcome pain and disability to lead more normal, happy lives.[117]

Couldn't the vision for investment firms be similarly stated? For example:

The story of men and women who have dedicated their lives and careers to helping people overcome financial challenges to achieve greater happiness.

Dan Pink, an expert on motivating knowledge workers, states unequivocally that "The most deeply motivated people – not to mention those who are most productive and satisfied – hitch their desires to a cause larger than themselves."[118]

Suzanne Duncan's paper on *Discovering Phi* asserts that the investment industry is high on passion but low on purpose. She calls the missing factor in the investment industry "phi" and writes:

Individuals with high phi are driven by a belief that they are working in the service of something larger than themselves. Their personal goals and values are aligned with those of their organization and their end clients. They are more likely to view their work as a calling rather than just a job.[119]

For Mackey, *purpose* is defined simply as the difference you are trying to make in the world. YELLOW leadership articulates a purpose larger than just beating the competition. Then YELLOW explains to all the workers what their role is in making this happen. "Beating the competition" is a means to the end. The investment industry must think more carefully about the true "end." FCG proposes that the true end is the well-being/happiness of ordinary people. Einstein said, "Such a loss of higher purpose is not uncommon today. Perfection of means and confusion of ends seem to characterize our age."[120] That describes exactly what has happened in the investment world: brilliant minds have collaborated to come up with wonderfully complex models – worthy of Nobel Prizes – that don't really help the common person. A global organization called The 300 Club, which is comprised of chief investment officers from the industry, cites complexity as one of the chief failings in the investment industry:

> Over reliance on complex financial models and structures will not deliver the holy grail – quite the reverse. There is an increasing belief that complex and expensive financial models and investment structures will deliver an improved outcome for investors. Whilst analytically this may look good on paper[,] there are severe limitations in the current thinking particularly when stressed by market dynamics which are likely to be increasingly atypical relative to market trends upon which these models and structures have been based. Added to this is the high level of structuring and investment cost buried in these structures which will invariably lead to relatively poor performance, irrespective of the market outcome.[121]

FCG's research reveals that investment firms – true to their heavy ORANGE origins – are showing little GREEN emphasis in their value systems. Yes, the *P&I* "Best Places" survey indicates much stronger interest in culture and teamwork, but the survey data we see weekly still show heavy emphasis on competition, achievement, and growth. FCG's prediction would be that values in the investment industry will shift over time to reflect the "Best Places" emphasis on culture, caring, community, environment, and the well-being of employees. The challenge for investment leaders is to become more YELLOW in their mindset so that they truly value and leverage the best of BLUE, ORANGE, and GREEN. Again, this is YELLOW's ability to think "both/and" rather than "either/or."

Mackey at Whole Foods is offered as one example of YELLOW leadership, but there are other good examples cited in the book *Firms of Endearment* by Sisodia, Wolfe, and Sheth. They describe these firms in this way:

> Firms of Endearment (FoEs) take an expansive worldview. Instead of seeing the world in narrow, constricted terms, they see its infinite positive possibilities. They believe deeply in the possibility of a rising tide that raises all boats. [The ongoing theme of "abundance," everyone can win.] Faced with a competitive threat, they

don't look to cut prices and costs and employees, but to add greater value. [Again, that's a big message is this book: investment firms must add actual value for the clients. For active investment firms, they must provide superior returns to earn an active fee. They should not hide behind greater complexity that clients simply don't understand.]

FoEs are bathed in the glow of timeless wisdom. Their "softness" in a hard world comes not because they are weak or lack courage, but from their leaders' knowledge of self, psychological maturity [that is, moving up the Maslow hierarchy and embracing YELLOW skillsets], and magnanimity of the soul. These companies are forceful and resolute in standing up for their principles. FoE leaders have the courage to defend and act decisively on their convictions.[122]

Table 7.1 Examples of FoE Companies and Their Leaders

Leader	Company
Jeff Bezos	Amazon
Jim Sinegal	Costco
Jim Goodnight	SAS Institute
Sergey Brin, Larry Page	Google
Barry and Eliot Tatelman	Jordan's Furniture
Jim and Anne Davis	New Balance
Herb Kelleher	Southwest Airlines
Jeff Swartz	Timberland
John Mackey, Walter Robb	Whole Foods
Kip Tindell	The Container Store
Ron Shaich	Panera
Bob Chapman	Barry-Wehmiller
Danny Meyer	Union Square Hospitality Group
Yusaf Hamied	Cipla
Terri Kelly	W. L. Gore

Costco offers a great example of the difference between "scarcity" and "abundance" thinking. Wall Street analysts have criticized Costco for overpaying its workers. (In fact, it does pay workers a higher-than-average industry wage.) Wall Street argues, from a scarcity mentality, that this strategy is ripping off shareholders. But, in fact, the stock price of Costco has rewarded shareholders handsomely. Why? Because the way Costco treats its workers – partly reflected in higher pay – leads to better service, higher morale, less turnover and – wait for it – better profitability. This is the YELLOW mindset at work, combining the best of both worlds: ORANGE strategy and efficiency with GREEN humanism.

The culture of an FoE tends to embrace the following values:

• Learning

• Trust

• Interconnectedness and interdependence [a major issue with investment firms that FCG is often asked to help with is "silos"]

• Integrity and transparency

• Loyalty

• Respect

• Belonging and oneness (the second level up in the Maslow hierarchy)

• Caring

• Fun

So, how does a BLUE, ORANGE, or GREEN leader become more YELLOW in his or her leadership? It seems like a rather vague skillset, one of those "I-know-it-when-I-see-it" kind. Fortunately, there is a body of knowledge and a curriculum for leaders who want to become YELLOW. Cindy Wigglesworth, a business professional with 20 years at Exxon/Mobil and a self-professed "engineer's mindset," became fascinated with this topic and created an assessment and training for spiritual intelligence (SQ). She is very good at simplifying complex subjects. She explained SQ in this way:

> The strong suit for ORANGE mindsets is their clever minds, or IQ. GREEN excels at emotional intelligence, or EQ, and YELLOW is characterized by SQ.[123]

In her book, *SQ 21: The Twenty-One Skills of Spiritual Intelligence*, she describes the skills that define SQ and how an individual can learn them. John Mackey wrote, in the foreword to her book: "I love this book. I haven't just read it – I have studied it and I have practiced it. I think the ideas in here are crucial for anyone who wants to grow wiser, more compassionate and to help create a better future."[124]

So, what is the definition of SQ? Wigglesworth describes it as "the ability to behave with wisdom and compassion, while maintaining inner and outer peace, regardless of the situation."[125] This definition is similar to Buffett's statement that temperament is more important than IQ for investment success. Given all the research on behavioral biases and how they interfere with good decision making, it seems only natural that investment leaders would want to achieve this level of equanimity. Her curriculum is devoid of any religious orientation, and some of the graduates would describe themselves as atheists. The core distinction she works with is the same one that Maslow addresses: the deficiency needs and the growth needs. People with high SQ understand that we all have an Ego and a Higher Self. Ego helps us survive and satisfy the deficiency needs, while the Higher Self wants to achieve the growth needs: purpose, service, and connection. Maslow states this dynamic in a straightforward way: "A hungry man may willingly surrender his need for self-respect in order to stay alive; but once he can feed, shelter, and clothe himself, he becomes likely to seek higher needs."[126] High SQ leaders have matured to the level where the Higher Self is in charge, and Ego is in service to it. Far too many investment leaders – leaders from all industries, for that matter – are run by their Egos. Wigglesworth uses a car analogy to make this point. She asks, "Who is driving your life? Spiritual Intelligence allows you to shift from being driven by the small-minded, short-sighted Ego to being driven by the big-hearted, forward-thinking Higher Self."[127]

Perhaps you begin to see why we place such importance on YELLOW leadership. It serves as the calm and mature intelligence that appreciates BLUE, ORANGE, and GREEN talents and knows the role of each. As Stephen Covey wrote, "Spiritual intelligence is the central and most fundamental of all the intelligences, because it becomes the source of guidance for the others."[128]

ORANGE readers may be wondering: But does it work? Does YELLOW leadership provide more success? Do FoE companies – which we assume have more YELLOW in their leadership – produce competitive returns? We asked the statistical experts at Bridgeway Capital Management (BCM, a quant firm) to analyze the returns of the FoE companies since the book was first published in 2007. Their analysis of the paper portfolio of FoE companies revealed the following:

1. The 18 FoE firms identified in 2007 outperformed the S&P 500 over the next 9 years.
2. The outperformance was consistent over time (not one big year).
3. The strong performance decayed over time (suggesting that there was something "going on" with these firms, which the market identified).[129]

BCM researchers were careful to point out that these results are not definitive proof that FoEs will continue to outperform. However, we can say with assurance that during the decade following the publication of the book, investors would not have suffered weak returns by investing in these socially conscious companies. FCG's view is that YELLOW leadership may well contribute to better performance over the long term. Time will tell.

YELLOW is a newly emerging mindset that is equipped to handle the complexities of the New Era. As GREEN emerges within the once-dominant ORANGE investment world, the YELLOW leaders are best equipped to deal with all the changing variables: millennials who want more recognition, feedback, and purpose; clients who desire a new value proposition; employees who expect more autonomy, transparency, and empowerment; shareholders who still demand a fair return; and the general public which doesn't trust the industry. YELLOW succeeds by appreciating the strengths of all the previous mindsets, and operates around the principle of "transcend and include," NOT transcend then dismiss. BLUE, ORANGE, and GREEN all have their place in a highly functioning organization. YELLOW translates into the Maslow hierarchy as greater consciousness, that is, operating at all levels of the hierarchy: Making sure that deficiency needs (security, community, and mastery) are met, while also ensuring that the growth needs (purpose, service, and making a difference) are met. No easy feat, to be sure. What we've tried to do in this chapter is describe the YELLOW leadership traits and values and give examples from the world at large.

Figure 7.1 summarizes some of the key points we've made about the investment industry:

- The investment industry is currently near the bottom of the Edelman Trust Barometer.

- Much of the industry is characterized by the ORANGE mindset, for both the asset managers and the intermediaries.

- Most of the industry's resources (60%) are aimed at alpha creation.

- Most investment professionals are still operating in the lower half of Maslow's hierarchy – the "deficiency needs" – rather than the "growth needs" at the top.

- The main focus of mission/vision statements is on clients, rather than all the stakeholders: clients, employees, owners, and society.

- What we'll do in a later chapter is show how YELLOW is appearing in the investment world. First, though, we want to cover an important topic that constantly trips up investment firms: blindspots.

Figure 7.1 Investment Management Ecosystem – Current: 2017

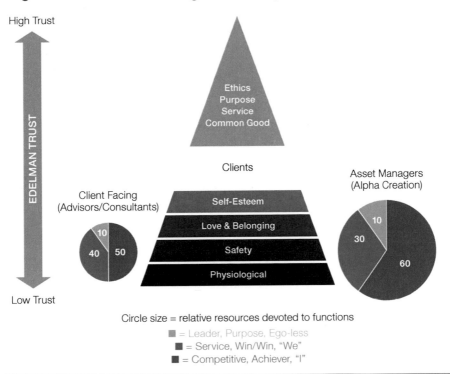

Circle size = relative resources devoted to functions

■ = Leader, Purpose, Ego-less
■ = Service, Win/Win, "We"
■ = Competitive, Achiever, "I"

Summary:

• YELLOW is the mindset that emerges "above" all the other mindsets. It transcends and includes all the other mindsets.

• In YELLOW the Higher Self is in charge, as opposed to the Ego, which dominates in the other mindsets.

• YELLOW has met the deficiency needs and aspires to satisfy the growth needs at the top of Maslow's hierarchy: purpose, service, and greater good.

• John Mackey, CEO of Whole Foods, is one example of a YELLOW-like leader.

• YELLOW can be thought of as spiritual intelligence (SQ), defined as combining wisdom and compassion. In contrast, ORANGE is high IQ, and GREEN is high EQ.

• Cindy Wigglesworth has designed an assessment and curriculum to measure and develop SQ for leaders.

---

[101] https://www.google.com/#q=conscious+leadership. A very good book on conscious leadership was written by former FCG partner, Jim Dethmer: Jim Dethmer, Diana Chapman, & Kaley Warner Clemp, The 15 Commitments of Conscious Leadership (Conscious Leadership Group, 2014); www.amazon.com/15-Commitments-Conscious-Leadership-Sustainable/dp/0990976904

[102] Theresa Shaffer, "Key Characteristics of Conscious Leaders," in *Business Compassion Reader;* http://voiceseducation.org/node/7286

[103] John Mackey & Rajendra Sisodia, *Conscious Capitalism* (Boston: Harvard Business School Publishing, 2014), p. 4.

[104] *Ibid.,* p. 14.

[105] Mick Jagger captured this nicely in the lyrics to "Angie": *With no lovin' in our souls / And no money in our coats, You can't say we're satisfied.* Hard to be happy when you're lonely or broke!

[106] Mackey & Sisodia, *Conscious Capitalism,* p. 16.

[107] *Ibid.,* p. 17.

[108] Ellis, *Index Revolution,* p. 147.

[109] *Ibid.,* p. 21.

[110] *Ibid.,* p. 28.

[111] *Ibid.,* p. 29.

[112] Duncan, *Discovering Phi.*

[113] *Ibid.,* p. 31.

[114] Fred cares so deeply about clients that he has organized and personally funded a conference for October 5, 2017, solely devoted to advisor/client relationships. Speakers include Charley Ellis and Suzanne Duncan, quoted throughout this book.

[115] For more on Ariel's commitment, go its website: https://www.arielinvestments.com/

[116] Larry Fink, Annual shareholder letter (April 10, 2016); https://www.blackrock.com/corporate/en-us/literature/press-release/larry-fink-chairmans-letter-to-shareholders-2016.pdf

[117] Mackey & Sisodia, *Conscious Capitalism,* p. 45.

[118] Pink, *DRIVE,* p. 131.

[119] Duncan, *Discovering Phi,* p. 25. Our colleague Michael Falk has devoted himself to positively influencing the financial lives of as many people as he can, and to that end has written a fine book with the CFA Research Foundation on solutions: www.letsalllearnhowtofish.com

[120] Mackey & Sisodia, *Conscious Capitalism,* p. 50.

[121] https://www.the300club.org/charter/

[122] Sisodia, Wolfe, & Sheth, *Firms of Endearment* (Saddle River,NJ: Pearson Education, 2014), pp. 22 23.

[123] Cindy Wigglesworth, personal communication, February 9, 2017.

[124] Mackey, "Foreword," in Cindy Wigglesworth, *SQ 21: The Twenty-One Skills of Spiritual Intelligence* (New York: SelectBooks, 2012), p. vii.

[125] *Ibid.,* p. vii.

[126] Quoted in Wigglesworth, *ibid.,* p. 23.

[127] *Ibid.,* p. 47.

[128] Quoted in *ibid.,* p. 31.

[129] FCG thanks John Montgomery and Christine Wang for their good work in analyzing the data.

CHAPTER EIGHT

Blindspots: Inconvenient Truths

A ll of the mindsets we've discussed – RED, BLUE, ORANGE, GREEN, and YELLOW – have blindspots. No question. However, because the investment industry is predominantly an ORANGE mindset, we'll look at the blindspots that are peculiar to that color. One of the strengths of the ORANGE mindset is its driving ambition. Type A, alpha-dog personalities are drawn to investments. The strengths are evident: strong work ethic, brilliant minds, creative strategies, focus, and a willingness to do "whatever it takes." But that's also a big weakness, which creates blindspots and bad behavior. When ORANGEs move into overdrive, their competitive nature can make winning the top goal. Otherwise decent and fair-minded people develop a blindness to their fiduciary responsibilities. The definition of *fiduciary* is clear:

> *A person who holds a legal or ethical relationship of trust with one or more parties. In a fiduciary relationship one person, in a position of vulnerability, justifiably invests confidence, good faith, reliance, and trust in another whose aid, advice or protect[ion] is sought in some matter. In such a relation, good conscience requires the fiduciary to act at all times for the sole benefit and interest of the one who trusts. A fiduciary duty is the highest standard of care for either equity or law.*[130]

This chapter explores the "dark" side of ORANGE. Anything overdone becomes a problem. When the healthy competitive juices of ORANGE are overdone, bad things happen. The client is no longer the top priority. Instead, profits, growth, and winning take precedence. With regard to fiduciary duties, FCG has seen major blindspots in these areas:

- **Ethics.** Despite the claim by all investment firms that they are behaving ethically, there are breaches, at the expense of the client.

- **Client-centrism.** Likewise, firms claim that they put clients first … but many don't.

- **Value proposition.** Many firms turn a blind eye to their basic value proposition: does it deliver value to the client?

Additionally, an ORANGE blindspot that can affect client well-being is:

- **Incentives and rewards.** As GREEN emerges in the investment industry, firms are saying the right things – like: "It's not all about the money." – but their reward systems still emphasize money.

Ethics

If a person lives long enough and makes enough predictions, invariably he gets one right. In 2000, Jim made a presentation to 13 people in a giant ballroom in Philadelphia at a CFA ethics conference. (In Boston that same week, there was standing room only at a tech conference.) Jim said to the little group that "the more frequent and reprehensible the conduct is in the industry, the more likely that the government will step in and impose regulations. Wise investment professionals, for the sake of the industry, will support CFA Institute [then AIMR] in its goal of 'setting a higher standard' and enforcing it."[131]

Jim got that one pretty much right (even a blind squirrel …) Due to numerous ethical violations, investment firms all around the world are dealing with more compliance and legal regulations than ever before. The largest "sludge" factor[132] in our culture surveys of investment firms is "slow moving/reactive." Much of this is explained by self-imposed regulation.

Nearly 17 years later, we now understand much better why the industry ignored ethical warnings then and still ignores them today: The ORANGE mindset wants to win and will rationalize bad behavior in doing so. As we said at the outset of this book, we are not suggesting that ORANGE is unethical and the other mindsets are saintly. All mindsets face their own unique temptations and have their weak moments. We are focusing on ORANGE because it dominates the investment world.

Consider the data that Jim collected while speaking to investment audiences in Australia. He made presentations on ethics to the CFA Societies of Melbourne and Sydney. Arguably, the audiences were reasonable proxies for the global investment profession – in other words, his findings are not evidence of an exclusively Australian phenomenon.[133]

As part of those presentations, Jim posed a series of questions about professional ethics to those in attendance (a total of 52 investment professionals in Melbourne and 56 in Sydney). First, he showed them examples of nine common ethical violations that FCG has identified as industry problems based on conversations with clients. The violations fall into the following categories:

1. selective presentation of performance numbers
2. spinning personnel changes
3. hiding salient performance-record features
4. misrepresenting the PM in charge
5. high-load funds
6. use of pitch books
7. use of sponsored conferences
8. capacity versus alpha
9. claims that performance "will soon return to normal"

From this list, the audiences responded that "performance presentation" and "personnel changes" were the two dominant categories of breaches. First, regarding performance, a fund's worst period of performance is omitted from presentations in favor of the time period over which its performance looks the strongest (usually three years, five years, or the last quarter). The manager does this to prevent the client from seeing all the facts. Virtually every manager has a graph or table in which its fund's performance looks strong and robust. Second, regarding personnel changes, employees "no longer with the company" are often portrayed as "non-team, weak players" instead of the key contributors they actually were. This fudge also occurs when a manager describes personnel changes that have occurred over time, especially when competitors poach his top performers. Note that these actions don't necessarily harm the clients – perhaps the manager will win the client and perform well – but the behavior is not ethical or trustworthy.

Jim then asked the participants, "Do you agree that the prior list [i.e., the information he had just shown them] contains examples of ethical breaches?" And 100% of the attendees in Melbourne and Sydney said yes. When asked, "Do you believe that investment firms routinely commit these breaches?" 93% and 81% respectively responded in the affirmative.

Finally, "Do you believe that *your* firm committed any of these breaches in 2009?" Jim had already carefully defined the ethical actions and walked them through the steps of (1) Are these breaches? "Yes." and then (2) Do they occur in the industry? Largely "yes." The professionals in each audience saw through their blindspots and two-thirds of them said, "Yes, those breaches occur at our firm." At the time, we found this response remarkable. More than half of the CFAs in each room were saying, "Yes, those activities are unethical and yes, our firm does them." But now, with a much better understanding of the ORANGE mindset, we understand it. Of course, understanding it doesn't make it right, but it helps explain why the Edelman Trust Barometer has the asset management business near the bottom. ORANGE on overdrive will run roughshod over ethics to win the prize.

Fortunately, FCG has worked with many investment firms recently whose leaders have embraced the ethical stance advocated by the CFA Institute. As GREEN and YELLOW mindsets become more prevalent in the industry, there is every reason to hope that overzealous ORANGE will contribute from its strengths and shore up its weaknesses.

Client-Centrism

Another blindspot in the investment world is the claim that clients come first: that is, that we have a fiduciary role. We touched on this earlier, but now we're addressing it head on. Duncan's research reveals the following:

> *This is an environment that measures success through competition, comparison, and contingent rewards; resulting in a culture that often prioritizes self-interest. Indeed, nearly two-thirds (65%) of investment professionals believe that their organization is acting in its own best interest rather than the client's.*[134]

FCG has found similar evidence. Despite Duncan's data cited here, CEOs maintain the view that their firm is truly placing the client first. While speaking at a conference in Canada, we collected some data on this topic. Figure 8.1 shows the vote from a room full of investment leaders.

Figure 8.1 Which stakeholder is top priority at your firm?

More than 70% of this audience dutifully answered with the politically correct answer: clients.

Indeed, if we review the hundreds of culture surveys FCG has done for asset management firms, the top value chosen is "client satisfaction" as seen from the following numbers:

1. Client satisfaction – 44%[135]

2. Professional – 42%

3. Ethical/Integrity – 38%

4. Collaboration/Teamwork – 37%

In the culture surveys that FCG conducts with asset managers, we find some shocking results. Employees are shown a list of 73 values/behaviors that are common in the investment world – like the ones shown above – and asked "Which ones currently exist in your firm? And, which ones would you like to see at your firm?" Simply put, which ones do you "have" and which ones would you "want"? It is not uncommon for FCG to see results in which "client satisfaction" does not show up in either the "have" or "want" list. For example, Figure 8.2 shows a survey result from a well-known firm in North America.

Figure 8.2 Top 10 Values – Aspirational Culture: Which values/behaviors best describe your preferred culture, that is, the one that would best allow the firm to realize its vision of success?

N = 57	Number of Responses	XYZ Percent	Industry Percent
Excellence/Continuous Improvement	**29**	**51%**	**41%**
Professional	**23**	**40%**	**33%**
Respect	**23**	**40%**	**23%**
Passion/Energy/Motivate	**23**	**40%**	**21%**
Ethical/Integrity	**21**	**37%**	**39%**
Long Term Perspective/Vision	**20**	**35%**	**43%**
Competitive/Win/Be the Best	**20**	**35%**	**15%**
Collaboration/Teamwork	**19**	**33%**	**41%**
Intelligent	**19**	**33%**	**26%**
Entrepreneurial Meritocracy tied	**18**	**32%**	**21%**

"Client satisfaction" does not make the list. Can you imagine the CEO of this firm sharing these results with clients?! That would be an awkward moment. No doubt some fine values were chosen by the staff – excellence, professional, integrity, collaboration, and so on – but the client would still be left wondering, "Why are *we* not showing up in the voting?"

The result shown in Figure 8.2 is not uncommon … so much for fiduciary responsibility. Duncan at State Street asked the same question of retail investors, and they agreed: "more than half (54%) of respondents believe that financial institutions are most likely to offer products and services in the firm's own best interest versus that of the client."[136]

State Street sums up its research by saying:

There is a disparity between the purpose we say we have on our websites and corporate messaging (helping clients meet their goals), and the purpose evident in our actions (competition and outperformance for its own sake).[137]

Based on these results, it would be easy to judge the asset management business harshly. But, again, that's why spiral dynamics is a useful framework. The ORANGE mindset drives for growth, success, and profit. It's arguably not well suited to a fiduciary role. It doesn't come naturally for ORANGE to put someone else's interest first. Foxes are not suited to caring for hens. Once we appreciate this, we can position ORANGE for success rather than setting it up for defeat and then blaming it.

Even more intriguing is this result from the sales team at a different investment firm (Figure 8.3). This is the group of people who are specifically called on to find clients and take good care of them!

Figure 8.3 Aspirational Culture.

N = 21	Number of Responses	ABC Percent
Accountability/Responsibility	9	43%
Commitment	9	43%
Professional	9	43%
Ethical/Integrity	8	38%
Collaboration/Teamwork	8	38%
Excellence/Continuous Improvement	7	33%
Results Oriented	7	33%
Candor/Honesty/Open	7	33%
Clear Performance Goals	6	29%
Expense Control Competitive/Win/Be the Best, Positive tied	6	29%

How is it possible that the sales and client facing people are not choosing "client satisfaction" in their aspirational view of the firm? (Pause for head scratching ...)

Raising people's awareness concerning blindspots can do a lot of good toward eliminating those blindspots. After all, the ORANGE mindset types are extremely smart and quite devoted to seeking the truth. So, when you present them with data, they can begin to see through their denial. The Canadian audience mentioned earlier, after some discussion, voted this way on the question: Have there been some times when clients did NOT come first? (See Figure 8.4.)

Figure 8.4 Moment of Truth: At our firm, there have been some times when clients did not come first.

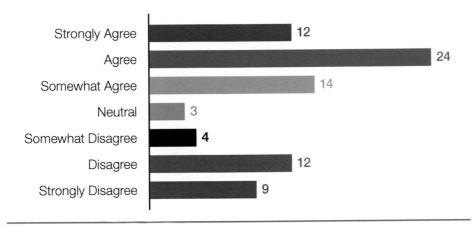

From the same audience that responded 70% that clients were the top priority, more than two-thirds in this vote said, "Well, actually, they don't always come first!"

With the ORANGE mindset's devotion to success, growth, and profit, it can be hard for them to truly move from a profit mindset to a client-centric one. Our work with investment firms has identified these examples of the two mindsets (Table 8.1).

Table 8.1 Two Different Mindsets

Client-Centric Mindset	Profit Mindset
1. Performance	1. Asset gathering
2. Closing funds	2. Keeping funds open
3. Fees aligned with performance (fair)	3. Fees indifferent to performance (max)
4. Solution-oriented; refer clients to best solution (custom)	4. Sell hot products, create funds to take it all (scale)
5. Investment process and teams are top-notch	5. Investment engine is broken, but still promoted to clients

Discussing them in order:

1. Are the leaders focused on delivering results for the clients, first and foremost, or do they lean toward gathering assets? An example of this occurred in a firm in which the CEO was very sales-minded and was always looking for opportunities to grow. His CIO told him, "We should close our flagship fund. It has reached capacity." The CIO thought they had reached an agreement: no more new assets. Within a week, the CEO met with a client who wanted to add $200 million to the flagship fund. At first the CEO held the line and said, "No." Then the moment of truth arrived. The client said, "OK, how about $400 million?" The CEO's response: "Done!" Later that year, the CIO left the firm, citing that incident as the "straw that broke the camel's back."

2. A different firm had grown its flagship fund to a sizable level. FCG asked the CIO of the firm, "What is the optimal size of this fund?" The response: about half of its current level. Again, if the client is really the top priority, then this fund should have been closed long ago.

3. The fee question is increasingly relevant. Baillee Gifford in Scotland has lowered fees in various products simply because they thought it was the right thing to do.[138] Contrast that decision with that of a CEO in London who asked his lead salesman to continue charging 100 basis points for a product that was getting roughly half that fee in the market. The sales person – clearly of high integrity – quit, stating, "I don't want my legacy to be: 'He over-charged the clients for as long as he could.'"

4. The idea here is that if you really place the client first, you will look for best solutions – even if that means referring the client elsewhere. One of FCG's Focus Elite firms[139] has done this, so don't shake your head and say, "Well, in the real world that would never happen." It does. Because the firm in question really believes that the only way to build absolute trust with clients is to always give them the best deal. The opposite extreme is to promote "hot dot" products that inevitably will collapse, hurting the client and proving the wonderful graphic by Carl Richards (Figure 8.5).

Figure 8.5

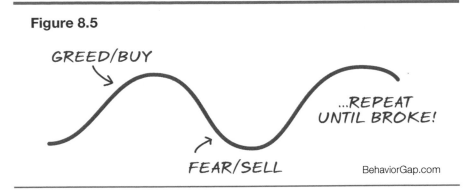

GREED/BUY

...REPEAT
UNTIL BROKE!

FEAR/SELL

BehaviorGap.com

5. The firms with high integrity and client-first mindset work tirelessly to keep their investment teams and processes in top shape. Therefore, they can promote the products in good conscience. Conversely, FCG has worked with investment teams that are broken – by their own admission – but are still being actively marketed by the firm to consultants and clients. Can these firms honestly say, "Clients come first"?

Returning to our original point about blindspots, FCG maintains that many investment firms have a blindspot around being client-centric. These firms are run by good people with good intentions, no question there. But, like the professionals who say, "My top priority is my family" and then spend nearly all their time working, there is a disconnect between what they say and what they do. There is a values clash. These professionals want to succeed at work – which requires time and effort – but they also wants to be good spouses and parents. Balance is required, and often some tough choices. Likewise, the investment firm that wants to be client-centric must find the balance between serving its various stakeholders. The first step in finding the right balance is to recognize the blindspot: that we are often placing commercial success (i.e., profit) ahead of client interests.

To put an exclamation point on this blindspot, consider this real example. FCG was asked to facilitate a strategic planning meeting for a large asset manager. The entire senior executive team was invited, including their heads of retail, institutional, and client relations. The meeting progressed into the afternoon and much was discussed about products, new channels, markets, investment results, profit margins, and a vision of the future. Not once was the client mentioned, in more than 5 hours of dialogue. At this point FCG stopped the meeting and highlighted this fact. The room fell as silent as if we had placed the proverbial turd in the punchbowl. Jim moved an empty chair up to the table and said, "Great, now let's finish this day as if the client is sitting right here." Suffice it to say, the discussion took a much different and more enlightened direction.

So, what's to be done? FCG recommends that investment leaders eliminate the blindspot by making client-first a regular topic at meetings and strategy sessions. Encourage staff members to filter every decision through the "client-first" value. Also, encourage all team members to practice empathy: how will the client view this decision? If you wish, use our "empty-chair" technique to remind them of their fiduciary duty. Use the empty chair as a way to start playing the devil's advocate. Ask the hard questions from the clients' point of view. Would clients sitting in that chair applaud your efforts to provide them with value? Or would they question your decisions from a fiduciary perspective? Illuminating the blindspot will not eliminate all tough choices, but it will bring integrity to the process. It will make for a clear-eyed view of all the options. Finally, we hope it will remind all investment professionals that they have a noble, fiduciary calling: to protect and serve their clients.

Value Proposition

The blindspot around value is a tricky one. The people mentioned in the *P&I* "Best Places" article are without doubt hardworking, smart, and well-intentioned. They work for reputable firms that consider themselves good citizens in the investment community. But let's not forget the wonderfully powerful observation of Sinclair Lewis, mentioned earlier:

> It is difficult to get a man to understand something, when his salary depends on his not understanding it.[140]

These people are mostly working at active management shops, and we've seen the data on fund performance at active shops. Not good. Bogle, Ellis, Swedroe, and others have made the case that fewer and fewer fund managers outperform consistently. Due to their active fees and underperformance, "Warren Buffett intensified his attacks on Wall Street money managers, saying that investors wasted more than $100 billion over the last decade on expensive advice."[141]

The ORANGE view tends to make us myopically interested in competing and winning, whereas the YELLOW view looks at the whole picture. YELLOW asks the question: "Collectively, is the investment industry delivering value to the population of investors at large?" Keeping the argument simple, we can compare the investment industry to, say, the medical industry. Are people healthier than they were 100 years ago? The answer is arguably yes. An obvious data point is life expectancy. People are living much longer. Jim's dear old mother, aged 94, simply wouldn't be alive if it weren't for all the medications available, as well as the surgery that repaired her heart. Or take another industry, like automobiles. Are the cars we're driving safer and better than 50 years ago? Without a doubt, yes. And soon we may be experiencing the miracle of driverless cars. (Jim's mother is a strong advocate for this, as she wants to be driving once again.) Yet another example, take the insurance industry. The industry aggregates risk and allows us to protect ourselves from catastrophic losses like our houses burning down, serious car accidents involving liabilities, or death of a breadwinner. In all of these cases, we can debate the fairness of the price we pay – the value – but overall, we would argue that society benefits from the products and services of the industries in question.

It's a fair question to ask: Has the average citizen who works, pays taxes, and saves for retirement benefited from the investment industry? Well, yes, in that markets rise over time and compound interest is the "eighth wonder of the world."[142] But has the investment industry helped people harness this power and use it most effectively? Arguably, no. The data shown earlier on retirement indicate that the majority of people in the United States – and many other developed countries – are not prepared for retirement, especially in light of their longer life spans. If the investment industry were working well on a collective level, the counsel given to clients combined with prudent and fairly priced services would help prepare them for a decent quality of financial life into retirement. The ORANGE mentality, which works wonderfully in competitive environments (producing better cars or smartphones) doesn't work in the investment industry. Yes, the competition does help market efficiency, but in doing so it reduces alpha – and as Duncan stated, 60% of the industry's resources are still devoted to that activity. For the industry to provide societal value, the mindset has to shift in three ways:

1. The industry needs to shift from "competitive" to "service" in nature. Price discovery will remain a function of the industry, helping to keep markets efficient and properly allocating capital. But the main job of the industry is to help people achieve financial well-being: that is, happiness involving a secure retirement.

2. The industry needs to align around a purpose statement that serves this function, something like: helping to positively influence people's financial well-being. This shift involves moving from performance/benchmark beating to outcomes for the clients. Are you helping to achieve happiness for your clients? They don't care about all the details of beta, alpha, benchmarks, Brexit, currency hedging, and so on. They want to know: Am I okay financially?

3. The industry needs to shift to YELLOW leadership which acknowledges that win/win/win/win solutions are indeed achievable. In the investment world, this looks like all stakeholders winning.

    a. Employees win by working for excellent firms that provide development and a sense of pride

    b. Clients win by gaining peace of mind around their finances

    c. Shareholders win by making reasonable profits

    d. Society wins because collectively people can retire with dignity and security, and markets are efficient, with capital allocated appropriately

Stating it again, the investment industry operates much like a casino, which is not a win/win/win. Rather, a few lucky casino players hit the jackpot and walk away as winners, while most players lose. Of course, the house is the consistent winner over time. This is basically the profit model for the industry: whatever the collective AUM is for all investors, the investment profession takes its fixed percentage; call it 1%. The investment industry is the house, it gets 1% of assets, year after year, regardless of performance. How else can you explain the incredible profitability of the industry? It's certainly not because the industry has delivered value! And as if this pricing scheme wasn't good enough, the truly ORANGE mindset of the hedge funds dreamed up an even better pricing model: 2 and 20! A recent *P&I* headline read, "Hedge Funds at the crossroads: offer alpha or disappear."[143]

Again, our intention is not to vilify ORANGE. ORANGE is doing what ORANGE naturally does. However, the blindspot allows the foxes to be in charge of the henhouse, and finally the hens are showing – via Edelman and other surveys – that they are not too thrilled with this arrangement. (At least at casinos, the losers get the entertainment value of playing the various games of chance, and a few free drinks! There is *no* entertainment value in paying a hefty fee and underperforming the index.)

At the core of the value proposition is the fee arrangement: a fair price for services rendered. Increasingly, investment firms are responding to the pressures to offer transparent and fair fees. Morningstar has been researching the relationship between fees and performance in mutual funds for years and found that: "Expense ratios consistently show predictive power. Using expense ratios to choose funds helped in every asset class and in every quintile from 2010 to 2015."[144]

Based on this awareness that fees are critical to performance, Capital Group has started selling "clean shares, which unlike most mutual fund shares classes, do not include a distribution fee baked in."[145] Other firms are developing creative strategies around fees that include provisions for underperformance. Motif Investing offers this guarantee:

No Compromise Guarantee
We stand behind the performance of Motif Impact Portfolios. If, after the first year, the performance of the model portfolio with the values filter you select underperforms

the corresponding base portfolio by one percentage point or more, we will refund 100% of your subscription fees.[146]

The trend here is encouraging. Firms are embracing the concept of fair value. Fred Martin, CEO of Disciplined Growth Investors, is a champion for fair fees. He says, "Fees are critically important. For example, if the advisor agrees to a long-term investment posture that honors client preferences but prudently reduces total portfolio performance, the advisor should charge lower fees than an unconstrained portfolio."[147]

Dan Solin has written some nice pieces on why the asset-based fee model won't survive. Here's an excerpt:

Congratulations. You've just landed a $5 million client who is nearing retirement. You reviewed her portfolio and recommended a different asset allocation. You presented her with a proposed portfolio of low-management-fee index funds, and carefully explained the historical risk and returns of this portfolio. You also prepared a comprehensive financial plan. It's a holistic plan that reviews all aspects of her financial life, including cash flow, debt strategies, rent versus buy analysis, investment analysis, insurance coverage, saving for retirement, when to take Social Security, withdrawal strategies, income tax strategies and an estate plan review, including family and charitable gifting ideas.

You provide an annual review to be sure the plan is being followed. You also rebalance the portfolio to keep her risk profile intact. Your asset-based fee for these services is 0.50% annually, which is $25,000 based on the present value of the portfolio. Over time, it's likely to increase.

If your client went to Vanguard directly and used its Personal Advisor Services, it would pay 0.30% annually ($15,000). The Vanguard advisor will create, according to Vanguard's web site, a "custom tailored financial plan," put the plan into action and manage the portfolio, while also working with the client to keep track of the plan's progress, and rebalance the portfolio when necessary.

An even more cost-effective option would be for the client to use a financial planner who will tell her exactly how to invest on her own, and will provide a financial plan for a fee. MainStreet Financial Planning is one of many advisors offering this service. MainStreet will prepare the comprehensive financial plan described above for an average fee of $4,200. It will include detailed investment recommendations the client can implement herself using Vanguard or another low-cost fund family. The fee includes assistance with implementation of the recommendations, free questions for 12 months, and a 6-month check-up session. Annual check-ups are $1,600. Portfolio rebalancing is available for $750 per session.

MainStreet is a member of the Garrett Planning Network. Members of this network are financial planners who are independently registered investment advisors and meet Garrett's participation standards. They agree to adhere to the CFP Board Code of Ethics and Practice Standards and the National Association of Personal Financial Advisors Fiduciary Oath. Many (like MainStreet) don't manage money and limit their services to the preparation of financial plans, on an hourly or flat fee basis. Just because there are lower-fee options available doesn't mean you have to match them. But, in this Internet age, your client is likely to uncover them, which can lead to an uncomfortable conversation – at best.

The availability of far more competitive alternatives raises other issues. How sound is a fee model that relies on the lack of knowledge of your clients about lower cost options? How comfortable are you advising your clients about the importance of keeping fees and costs low, while charging fees for financial planning that may be excessive? Is this consistent with your fiduciary obligation to your clients?[148]

You can see why ORANGE has turned a blind eye to these issues for years. There is no way around the conclusion that fair pricing will lead to lower margins for the industry. To the ORANGE mindset, this scenario is anathema. It's losing. It goes against the whole drive for growth, success, and profitability. GREEN and YELLOW are needed to recognize that this scenario is not losing if society is better off because people have largely achieved financial well-being and if trust in the industry is restored.

Incentives and Rewards

Another blindspot for investment ORANGE is motivation.[149] The industry still largely believes that throwing money at talent is the way to motivate those talented people. Despite the vast amount of research to the contrary, even the firms cited in "Best Places" – who have leaned into the GREEN mindset – often attempt to motivate via money. The ORANGE leaders have trained the industry to think this way. A simple study with children and reading illustrates this point. Two groups of children were asked to read books. One group was paid to do it. The other simply read for pleasure. Both groups successfully finished their reading assignments. The lesson came after the study was completed: The paid readers refused to read unless they were paid. The other (nonpaid) group continued reading because they had learned that reading was fun. The lesson was clear: If you train people to think that an activity is only worth doing if it is rewarded, then they'll insist on a reward. The key variable here is intrinsic versus extrinsic rewards. Intrinsically, reading is fun, so we naturally will do it, regardless of an extrinsic reward. But if we link reading to extrinsic rewards – like money – then we feel cheated if we aren't paid for it. The ORANGE investment world has trained a whole generation of workers to feel that investment work must be highly rewarded. This causal connection exists even though the number-one motivation for investment workers is "the nature of the work itself." We have talked to countless investment professionals who say, "This work is fascinating. I'd be doing it for myself even if I weren't paid anything." (In other words, investing their own funds privately would be satisfying.)

Dan Pink, Frederick Herzberg, Suzanne Duncan, and many other researchers have shown conclusively that a shift from extrinsic to intrinsic improves motivation. The biggest intrinsic motivators, as described earlier, are:

1. Purpose: doing something meaningful to make a difference
2. Autonomy: freedom to achieve the task in one's own chosen fashion
3. Mastery: continually improving, making progress towards greater excellence

The influx of millennials into the workforce will influence this shift from extrinsic to intrinsic rewards. Gallup describes it as "purpose over paycheck." Millennials are reflecting different mindsets from bright ORANGE about money.

Already there is a shift in why people stay in the industry. Per State Street's research,[150] "only 20% of our respondents indicated that compensation is the reason they remain in the industry." At an investment conference in 2016, leaders were asked, "If your compensation was cut in half, would you keep doing what you are doing, i.e. stay in the industry?"[151] More than two-thirds of the participants indicated yes, suggesting again that it's not about the money. FCG research suggests that the work itself – challenging and interesting – is the main motivator in the industry. New thinking about reward systems is necessary given this shift in thinking.

Why? Because the heavily ORANGE industry is preoccupied with competition, comparison, and the contingent rewards that result,[152] which create pressures that affect decision making. About half of all industry professionals worry about career risk, with "52% believing they would be fired after 18 months of underperformance. Among asset managers and wealth managers, 36% report that acting in the best interest of their client actually implied taking on career risk."[153]

And there you have a true blindspot: leaders who want to succeed reward their teams in ways that make them less likely to succeed.

So, what is the enlightened way to motivate? Dan Pink is on point when he writes, "Get compensation right, and get it off the table."[154] Don't focus on it. Find the right rewards package and then redirect workers' focus back to purpose, autonomy, and mastery, the intrinsic motivators. We use the term rewards in this context to include both the extrinsic and intrinsic rewards associated with the experience of working at a firm in a particular role. We have found that the key to success is applying a total rewards approach rather than simply a compensation approach.

Importantly, what does "right" mean in this context? FCG has done many compensation assignments in the industry and found that the way to get it "right" is to follow these guidelines:

- **Fair:** and that means in the eyes of the beholder (i.e., the worker)

- **Transparent:** not mysterious or subjective, but as objective and logical as possible and tied to a clear understanding of the firm's success

- **Simple:** easy to understand, because this builds trust

State Street uses a similar approach to getting it right, saying that the negative effects of compensation can be "mitigated if the compensation structure is perceived as fair, controllable, and transparent. However, only 44% of respondents in our study believe their compensation structure is fair, 40% believe it is transparent and 34% believe it is controllable."[155]

In our own research, we have learned that much of the dissatisfaction around fairness is more about the process (Fair, Transparent, and Simple assessment and communication) and less to do with the amount. For example, investment professionals (PMs and analysts) are far more interested in greater volatility in pay based on meritocracy, whereas operations professionals prefer less volatility and have a greater teamwork orientation. Our research shows that each group is driven by different intrinsic motivators and the reward (the extrinsic motivation) is simply one way to recognize the value they bring to the process.

So, how do you ensure "getting it right" in the eyes of those being rewarded by the system? After all, fairness, like beauty, is in the eye of the beholder. The simple but profound idea is that including workers in compensation discussions is crucial to getting it "right." The prevalent model in the industry is for firm leaders to meet with consultants, review the benchmarks for industry compensation, and then determine what the formula will be for their staff. The outcome is frequently a less-than-enthusiastic reception by staff members. The GREEN mindset, with its appreciation for consensus, is much more open to the FCG approach of including staff members in the compensation discussion. ORANGE balks at the fear of losing control.

Focus should be on rewards rather than compensation because the discussion with employees should be more far-reaching than just money. It should include the intrinsic factors – purpose, autonomy, mastery – and factors like ownership, flexibility, and pay as well. Actually, industry leaders of all mindset "colors" are beginning to understand the shift from compensation to rewards. As one asset management CFO said,

> *Remuneration is important, but it is no longer the most important factor. Before, payment was much more important but now autonomy and being a part of something bigger than yourself [purpose] is becoming even more important."*[156]

Because fairness is one of the measures of success, keep in mind that reward plans are shifting from "one size fits all" to being customized to fit the standard of the individual or team being rewarded. For example, to many employees greater autonomy or flexibility is as much of a reward as cash. For others, ownership is important, or being part of an opportunity to volunteer in the community. To some, development is a key reward … and the list goes on. YELLOW leaders recognize that as the workforce evolves, so must the firm's approach to rewards.

Let's consider examples of investment firms that are demonstrating success in the New Era by leveraging the strengths of the various mindsets. First, though, we'll ask Michael Falk, CFA, who is the most ORANGE member of the FCG team, if we've given a fair account of ORANGE in the book so far.

Summary:

- The ORANGE mindset, with all its wonderful strengths, has some powerful weaknesses and blindspots that powerfully affect the performance of fiduciary duties.

- Spiral dynamics helps us see the strong suits of ORANGE – strategy, ambition, and focus – but also its downside, when overdone: competitive, selfish, winning-at-all-costs.

- Four major blindspots for ORANGE are ethics, clients (fiduciary duties), value, and compensation.

- Both of our earlier models – Maslow and spiral dynamics – help us to understand why ORANGE leadership is insufficient by itself to lead in the future.

- As individuals move up the Maslow hierarchy, they naturally want more participation, autonomy, and purpose. Millennials are asking for this already.

---

130 https://en.wikipedia.org/wiki/Fiduciary

131 Jim Ware, "Drawing the Line Is a Gray Area," in *AIMR Conference Proceedings* 2002(2) (July 2000); http://www.cfapubs.org/doi/abs/10.2469/cp.v2000.n2.3002

132 "Sludge" represents behaviors driven by fear that slow down a firm: gossip, blame, manipulation, and so on.

133 A 2017 CFA global survey showed results similar to FCG's experience in Australia. So, no, the ethics issue is not unique to Australia! See https://twitter.com/Enterprising/status/825008883877842944

134 Duncan, *Discovering Phi*, p. 13.

135 Percent of respondents who chose this as a value in their firm's culture. Averaged over all the surveys FCG has done.

136 Duncan, *Discovering Phi*, p. 20.

137 *Ibid.*

138 Interestingly, the reaction from clients was a suspicious, "What's up? Why are they cutting fees?"

139 Nine firms that FCG has identified as having strong leadership and culture. For details about these firms, see our paper, "Linking Culture to Success," available at www.focuscgroup.com

140 http://www.goodreads.com/quotes/21810-it-is-difficult-to-get-a-man-to-understand-something

141 Nicole Friedman, *Wall Street Journal* (Feb. 26, 2017); www.wsj.com/articles/warren-buffett-has-no-doubt-on-passive-bet-1488037970

142 Albert Einstein: "Compound interest is the eighth wonder of the world. He who understands it, earns it ... he who doesn't ... pays it." http://www.goodreads.com/quotes/76863-compound-interest-is-the-eighth-wonder-of-the-world-he

143 Christine Williamson, "Firms at the Crossroads: Offer Alpha or Disappear," *Pensions&Investments* (March 6, 2017), p. 5; http://www.pionline.com/article/20170306/PRINT/303069984/firms-at-the-crossroads-offer-alpha-or-disappear

144 Russell Kinnell, "Predictive Power of Fees," *Morningstar*, p. 2.

145 https://www.ft.com/content/5e1df770-0d58-11e7-a88c-50ba212dce4d

146 https://www.motifinvesting.com/

147 Fred Martin, personal email communication to FCG, March 23, 2017.

148 Dan Solin, *Advisor Perspectives* (November 14, 2016).

149 To be fair, many mindsets – not just ORANGE – still face this issue: the belief that money is a good motivator for knowledge workers. One of our goals at FCG is to help the industry change its approach to incentives.

150 Duncan, *Discovering Phi*, p. 16.

151 Rosemont annual conference, November 2016, Philadelphia, PA.

152 Duncan, *Discovering Phi*, p. 17.

153 *Ibid.*

154 Pink, *DRIVE*, p. 134.

155 Duncan, *Discovering Phi*, p. 16.

156 *Ibid.*, 41.

CHAPTER NINE

Interlude: An ORANGE Perspective

I t's only fair to let Michael Falk, one of the authors of this book, a partner at FCG, and a card-carrying member of ORANGE, weigh in on his view of the book so far. We want to do this for several reasons:

1. ORANGE readers may feel that FCG is minimizing, or dismissing entirely, the importance of ORANGE. (That is not our intention.)
2. Readers may mistakenly infer that FCG is arguing for entirely passive strategies. (Not so.)
3. ORANGE readers may feel that their viewpoint is not fully represented in this GREEN-slanted view of the industry. (Not so. Our message advocates for a balanced approach.)

We think Michael is a credible advocate for the value of ORANGE. He was a CIO earlier in his career. He has been an active manager of a hedge fund. He is the author of a book on entitlement programs to promote economic growth.[157] His personality is INTJ (Myers-Briggs) and "5" on the Enneagram, which is very much the ORANGE personality type.

Jim: Michael, do you agree that you are an ORANGE mindset?

Michael: Very much so, though I've shifted over the years, which is what the book suggests many of us do as investment professionals. I'd say I started out as pure ORANGE. I am very competitive, and in my twenties I aspired to be a Major League baseball pitcher. I played semi-professional baseball for over a decade before deciding on a financial career. I love the markets and started my career as an investment advisor. After earning my CFA designation, I was a Chief Investment Officer for several years. Then I started a hedge fund which I managed up until my full-time role at FCG, where I handle investment process and strategy assignments.

Jim: Have you shifted away from pure ORANGE?

Michael: Yes. Life experiences and the "Maslow" maturation described in the book have added a GREEN and YELLOW component to my thinking. My father had a bad experience with his retirement planning. The company he was working for went bankrupt, so at 59 years of age, my dad found himself looking for a job because he wasn't able to retire. I experienced that deeply and decided that my professional purpose was "to positively influence as many people's financial lives as I could." In short, to help people. My recent book was motivated by that desire. It's the most purposeful thing I've done as a professional.

Jim: So, if you're no longer 100% ORANGE, where are you now?

Michael: Probably about 50% ORANGE, 30% GREEN, and 20% YELLOW. I'm still very competitive, love the markets, and the investment industry, but I'm able to see the benefits of GREEN – collaboration, win/win, and more "we" thinking – especially as I've worked with the FCG team, which is very GREEN. I think of GREEN as being more purpose driven and service minded. For me, YELLOW is an acknowledgment that I've become less Ego driven and more "larger-cause" motivated. My book, for example, is a direct statement of that change.

Jim: Do you agree with the characterization of ORANGE in this book?

Michael: Yes. ORANGE is competitive, hardworking, and driven to mastery and excellence. No question. And in my view, these factors contribute to the public welfare by:

- Encouraging price discovery

- Providing liquidity

- Properly allocating capital

- Contributing to overall market efficiency

Jim: What about the weaknesses – or blindspots – that we've cited in the book?

Michael: In my view, ORANGE can go to excess. In our work with clients, we've seen examples of greed and selfishness, and times when ORANGE became overconfident about its own abilities. For example, firms that are active investors and have underperformed for long periods of time, may continue without questioning the value they bring to clients. Supposedly, there is about $8 trillion of closet index funds charging active fees, and that is inappropriate. So, yes, unbridled ORANGE can go off the rails and do harm. That's why I like the message of this book: that ORANGE can be a powerful contributor when its passion is tied to purpose.

Jim: So, does the industry deserve the poor reputation shown in the Edelman Trust data?

Michael: Yes and no. There are ethical breaches and client-NOT-first episodes in the industry, which we've cited in the last chapter [Chapter 8]. But a lot of firms – ones that we work with – are doing a first-rate job, and you never hear about them. They are quietly going about the work of prudently and expertly advising their clients. And that's boring, so the media doesn't report on it.[158] Bernie Madoff and Wells Fargo grab the headlines. Plus, there are unseen benefits that society enjoys, like market efficiency, that most consumers never consider. So, are there issues? Yes. Can we do better? Yes. But is the track record a disaster? No. I think this book's message is important because it tries to leverage the benefits of ORANGE by encouraging more GREEN and YELLOW in the future.

Jim: What about financial advisors and consultants? Do they add value?

Michael: They can. The challenge for them is often career risk. A good financial advisor or consultant can add lots of value by educating and challenging the client. For example, an advisor might review a client's plan and say, "You need to spend less and save more." That would be appropriate push-back. But many advisors or consultants are driven by Maslow's deficiency needs – security, approval, and control – so they avoid giving the accurate and necessary advice and fall in line with the client's wishes.

Jim: Do you have more to say about the value of ORANGE?

Michael: Yes, lots more.

Jim: Would you like to cover that in an appendix?

Michael: For sure. Readers who would like to hear more from ORANGE, see the appendix [Appendix 1] and I'll give additional detail on the role of ORANGE in the future: Topics like fee structure, appropriate benchmarks, and finding win/win/win outcomes for all parties.

---

157 Falk, *Let's All Learn How to Fish…*
158 The tagline for Mawer Investment Management Ltd. in Calgary is "Be Boring. Make Money™."

CHAPTER TEN

Asset Management in the New Era: Elite Firms

G iven the natural and healthy skepticism of ORANGE, readers may be wondering, *Is this just pie-in-the-sky utopia? Is this just Plato writing about the ideal society in The Republic?* Well, partly yes. We don't think there are many full-blown YELLOW leadership teams in the asset management industry. However, there are teams that are manifesting some YELLOW, in the sense that they are skillfully using the different mindsets we've described in a successful way. Since 2012, FCG has been doing an annual identification of such firms and awarding them the distinction of "Focus Elite" status. These firms have worked hard to achieve excellence in leadership and culture – and, although financial success is not a criterion for selection, they happen to be profitable as well. For a list of these firms, and descriptions of their leadership and culture, see Appendixes 3 and 4 in this book, and our white paper, *Linking Culture to Success.*[159]

Let's examine a few of these firms. We'll start with Polen Capital, which was also a "Best Places to Work" winner in *P&I*. Polen is a classic boutique asset manager, located in Boca Raton, Florida, with 38 employees. They describe themselves in this way:

> *Polen Capital is a global independently-owned growth equity boutique, led by an experienced team of investment professionals who are committed to preserving and growing the assets of our clients through a prudent and disciplined long-term investment approach.*

> *Since 1989, our Investment Team has focused on identifying, monitoring and investing in only the highest quality growth businesses. Our prudent strategy is focused, first of all, on identifying innovative businesses that offer the greatest potential for sustainable, above-average earnings growth. From that select universe, we cull the few businesses that we believe possess the financial strength to weather the economic cycles with the least amount of market volatility.*

Our concentrated Focus Growth portfolio has a long-term outlook with an average investment holding period of approximately five years. Our Global Growth and International Growth strategies follow the same long-term, buy-to-hold approach. We support our investment management efforts with outstanding client service that is transparent, efficient and precise.

We offer both a Focus Growth strategy and a Global Growth strategy accessible through Separately Managed Accounts (SMAs), Mutual Funds and Undertakings for the Collective Investment of Transferable Securities (UCITS).[160]

Nothing unusual in this description, a classic long-only shop. On the ORANGE side of things, the firm is typical, as they put up excellent long-term numbers and have grown nicely. On the GREEN side of things, they have built a wonderfully collaborative and healthy culture. On the BLUE side, they have a strong back office and compliance operation that runs smoothly. And all of this has grown out of a very RED culture that their founder, David Polen, established years ago. Using FCG's culture survey to analyze the strength of their culture, the results are remarkably strong, arguably the best we've seen.

For starters, consider the firm's current culture, with the top values and behaviors shown in Figure 10.1.

Figure 10.1 Top 10 Values – Existing Culture:
Check the Values/behaviors that best describe your current culture.
(10 choices, 73 options)

N = 38	Number of Responses	Polen Percent	Industry Percent
Results Oriented	26	68%	30%
Excellence/Continuous Improvement	22	58%	24%
Client Satisfaction	22	58%	44%
Long Term Perspective/Vision	22	58%	23%
Collaboration/Teamwork	19	50%	36%
Ethical/Integrity	16	42%	38%
Community/Social Responsibility	16	42%	9%
Professional	16	42%	42%
Respect	13	34%	19%
Accountability/Responsibility Balance (Home/Work) tied	12	32%	25%

Green = Match between top existing and aspirational values. Shaded colors = 20% difference with industry.

Notice that the "big four" investment values – Clients, Ethics, Collaboration, Excellence – are all part of their current culture. This is the classic DNA of an investment firm. But also, notice that "Community/Social Responsibility" is added to the typical investment culture. This firm, like the "firms of endearment," serves all its stakeholders: clients, employees, owners, and the community/society. Also, note that "Long-Term Perspective/Vision" is alive and well at Polen. Leadership emphasizes the importance of a compelling, long-term vision. As Duncan points out in her Phi report, only "15% of professional investors strongly believe their leaders articulate a compelling vision."[161] Polen is leading from vision. Specifically, their mission and vision are:

Mission: Preserve and grow client assets to protect their present and enable their future.

Vision: To build a brand name investment management firm recognized for the quality of our people, our investment portfolios, and overall client experience.

Polen provides a great work environment for employees, who in turn provide great performance and service for the clients. The natural outcome of this attention to employees and clients is prosperity for the owners.

Next, look at the aspirational culture. As discussed earlier, FCG looks at both the "have" and "want" sides of a culture. They "have" the values/behaviors shown in Figure 10.1, and they "want" the values/behaviors shown in Figure 10.2.

Figure 10.2 Top 10 Values – Aspirational Culture: Check the Values/behaviors that best describe your preferred culture, that is, the one that would allow the organization to realize its vision of success. (10 choices, 61 options)

N = 38	Number of Responses	Polen Percent	Industry Percent
Balance (Home/Work)	23	61%	33%
Excellence/Continuous Improvement	18	47%	41%
Client Satisfaction	16	42%	38%
Collaboration/Teamwork	15	39%	43%
Leadership Development/Mentoring	14	37%	28%
Long-term Perspective/Vision	13	34%	36%
Ethical/Integrity	13	34%	34%
Results Oriented	12	32%	25%
Employee Empowerment	11	29%	21%
Loyalty Quality/Precision tied	11	29%	17%

Green = Match between top existing and aspirational values. Shaded colors = 20% difference with industry.

In this chart, notice that all the GREEN-colored values/behaviors appear as both "have" and "want." In our experience, this indicates a strong culture: a set of values/behaviors that is the same in both the "have" and "want" cultures. Two aspirational values/behaviors that are added to the "want" list are "Leadership Development/Mentoring" and "Employee Empowerment." As millennials enter the workforce and as ORANGE becomes more GREEN, all leaders are seeing these requests. (Even among the Focus Elite firms, the number-one gap between "have" and "want" is Leadership Development/Mentoring.)

FCG's survey also examines the Maslow deficiency needs (driven by fear). In her work, Duncan agrees that fear is a negative motivator.[162] (Figure 10.3).

Figure 10.3 Sludge Analysis

Total Respondents = 38		0%	10%
Sludge Factors	Number of Responses	Polen Percent	Industry Percent
Blame	0	0%	6%
Bureaucracy	0	0%	9%
Territorial	0	0%	12%
Defensive Behaviors	0	0%	12%
Disrespect	0	0%	3%
Entitlement	0	0%	7%
Gossip	0	0%	8%
Manipulation	0	0%	4%
Politics	0	0%	12%
Negative	0	0%	5%
Short-term Focus	0	0%	10%
Slow Moving/Reactive	0	0%	14%

By comparison, some poorly managed asset management firms will have 20% to 30% sludge in their culture. The chart in Figure 10.3 shows Polen and the industry average data. A positive culture pays huge dividends by driving fear out of the organization and thereby lowering the sludge factors. FCG wrote a paper with Jason Hsu, formerly the CIO at Research Affiliates, published in the *Journal of Portfolio Management*, which showed that blame is inversely correlated with performance.[163] Very simply, if you want better performance, reduce blame in the firm.

The next chart (Figure 10.4) shows how Polen ranks relative to the "Focus Elite" and the average investment firm in our database on typical indicators of success: factors like the ability to attract top talent, manage talent, communicate clearly, and execute on plans. Again, you see that Polen is outstanding in these areas.

Figure 10.4 Success Factors

Success Factors (N = 38)	% Agree			% Disagree		
As an organization, we have the ability to attract top talent.	100%	81%	93%	0%	10%	4%
We are free from silos in our organization.	79%	45%	48%	8%	33%	34%
We have strong talent management which includes career pathing and succession planning.	89%	49%	66%	0%	32%	19%
We have and ownership mentality, our employees think like owners of the business.	92%	60%	75%	3%	24%	11%
We are good at executing plans.	95%	70%	82%	3%	15%	11%
Our senior team communicates well (clear and transparent).	97%	65%	72%	3%	22%	15%
We have the resources to do our work well.	95%	79%	86%	5%	14%	9%

Black = The Focus Elite. Blue = Industry.
Agree = slightly agree, agree, strongly agree. Disagree = slightly disagree, disagree, strongly disagree.

The next chart (Figure 10.5) really tells the story of a "Best Places to Work" firm. Polen has complete and full engagement from its employees. (Polen is shown in gold in Figure 10.5.) Few other firm we've surveyed have this level of loyalty.

Figure 10.5 Loyalty Factor

Think about what level of financial incentive it would take for you to leave your current firm. Imagine if a firm like yours existed just down the street. Which of the following statements most closely describes your current attitude:

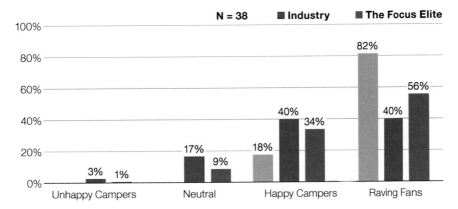

UNHAPPY CAMPERS: I might move for less money, I do not like the environment here. I would like an improvement in my working environment.

NEUTRAL: I might move for the same or slightly more money, if the other firm had a good reputation. It's not bad here, but I'm sure there are better work environments.

HAPPY CAMPER: I would require more money to move. Even if the other firm had a good reputation, I believe this firm does a lot of things right and I'm happy here.

RAVING FANS: I would require substantially more money to move. This firm has created an excellent work environment and I am loyal to it.

As we drill down deeper into Polen's results, we see that the leaders are creating a culture that includes purpose, autonomy, and transparency, three values that Duncan highlighted in her exploration of top motivators for the industry. First, look at Figure 10.6, showing that a higher purpose is what truly motivates the largest number of employees at Polen.

Figure 10.6 Motivation: Please choose the two factors that are the most meaningful in your daily experience.

N = 38	
The work serves a larger purpose, doing something positive in the world.	**18**
The work contributes to a sound and sustainable financial future for our firm.	**9**
The work benefits our clients, and I enjoy happy clients most of all about my job.	**17**
The work allows me to spend time with bright and engaging colleagues.	**15**
The work is interesting, challenging and intellectually stimulating.	**17**

This result was the first time FCG had seen "purpose" emerge as the top motivator for a firm. Usually, firms choose "work is interesting…" as the top motivator. While Duncan calls the industry "high in passion, low in purpose," Polen has achieved both: highly motivated employees working toward a meaningful goal. A big theme in this book is combining passion and purpose.

Next, look at the level of autonomy that workers have (Figure 10.7).

Figure 10.7 Professionals: Trusted vs. Managed

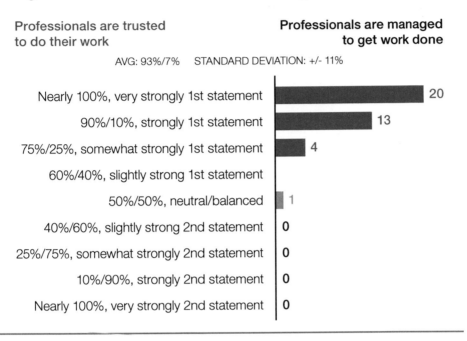

Professionals are trusted
to do their work

**Professionals are managed
to get work done**

AVG: 93%/7%   STANDARD DEVIATION: +/- 11%

Nearly 100%, very strongly 1st statement	20
90%/10%, strongly 1st statement	13
75%/25%, somewhat strongly 1st statement	4
60%/40%, slightly strong 1st statement	
50%/50%, neutral/balanced	1
40%/60%, slightly strong 2nd statement	0
25%/75%, somewhat strongly 2nd statement	0
10%/90%, strongly 2nd statement	0
Nearly 100%, very strongly 2nd statement	0

Workers at Polen are not micro-managed. They are trusted to get their work done as they see fit. This factor is very strong in motivating all workers, young and old alike.

Finally, consider the level of transparency. Are workers informed about key decisions and actions at the firm? Or are they kept in the dark? Our colleague Keith Robinson is fond of calling the latter management style "Trunk Management": leadership drives around with the workers in the car's trunk; they know they're going somewhere but have no idea where! Polen's workforce feels very informed about what's going on at the firm (Figure 10.8).

Figure 10.8 Favor: Transparency vs. Need to Know

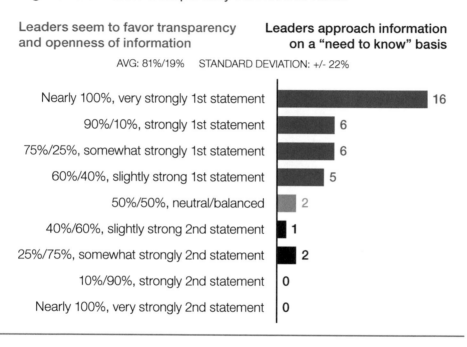

Leaders seem to favor transparency and openness of information — Leaders approach information on a "need to know" basis

AVG: 81%/19% STANDARD DEVIATION: +/- 22%

Nearly 100%, very strongly 1st statement	16
90%/10%, strongly 1st statement	6
75%/25%, somewhat strongly 1st statement	6
60%/40%, slightly strong 1st statement	5
50%/50%, neutral/balanced	2
40%/60%, slightly strong 2nd statement	1
25%/75%, somewhat strongly 2nd statement	2
10%/90%, strongly 2nd statement	0
Nearly 100%, very strongly 2nd statement	0

So, how is Polen able to create such a strong culture with a winning record? What is it about their leadership team that allows them to do this? Here is how Dan Davidowitz, CIO/PM, describes the firm's development:

Polen Capital's culture today is far different from what it was just 10 years ago. Back then, the firm's Founder/CEO, who called himself a benevolent dictator [RED in spiral dynamic terms], set a tone of underappreciation and sometimes even fear [thus activating the Ego around deficiency needs]. In a difficult period from 2005 2008, firm AUM declined nearly 90% due to a combination of weak relative performance and poor business decisions. But the three key lieutenants – led by then COO Stan Moss, who believed deeply in the investment philosophy and the team – decided that they would stick together and ride out the storm. Four years later, the founder passed away after a short, but difficult bout with cancer. The morning of Mr. Polen's passing, Moss who became CEO, gathered everyone together to discuss the difficulty the firm was about to endure. He asked for everyone to work together to get us to the other side. Today, the firm's 2nd generation leadership and culture are based on protecting and growing client assets, open and over-the-line communication and attracting and retaining the best talent in the industry. Today it is rare when someone is not "all in." And when that happens, they stand out and soon leave.[164]

The "key lieutenants" mentioned in this excerpt are Stan Moss, Dan Davidowitz, and Damon Ficklin. They are completely and passionately devoted to a larger purpose: taking care of all their stakeholders. As mentioned earlier, Polen posts photos of their clients in the break room, so all employees and visitors can see their faces. Second, the "key lieutenants" are a good balance of ORANGE, GREEN, and BLUE, each with emerging YELLOW. The CEO Moss has a classic ORANGE mindset but has excellent self-awareness and a commitment to increasing it. Davidowitz has a GREEN mindset – a bit unusual for that role – and also a high level of self-awareness. Ficklin is BLUE with high self-awareness.[165] They are a strong team, as they respect and trust each other and naturally provide checks and balances in decision making for the firm.

Finally, a note of hope from Polen's story for all asset managers. As recounted earlier, Polen was founded and managed in a heavy RED style. Having seen the effect of RED on the culture of the firm, the new leaders committed themselves to doing leadership differently. In this case, their history helped motivate them strongly to building a healthy and sustainable culture, and they have succeeded nicely. So, readers, take heart. If you think your culture is suboptimal, there are success stories – like Polen's – in which the leaders turned it around in fairly short order. We can also add that all of the Focus Elite firms went through their "dark night of the soul" in which they faced serious challenges that might have derailed them. There is no perfect firm with a blemish-free history. All the Focus Elite firms slayed their own dragons.

Consider another Focus Elite winner, Disciplined Growth Investors (DGI) in Minneapolis. Similar to Polen, DGI is a classic, long-only equities boutique. Under the leadership of Fred Martin, CEO, they have been diligently working on their culture for nearly 10 years now. The most recent three culture surveys for existing culture (the "haves") are shown in Figure 10.9. Remember, all the values/behaviors shown in GREEN are both "have" and "want" values/behaviors (i.e., they appear on both charts).

Figure 10.9 Yearly Comparisons: Existing Culture

April 2010 N = 15	February 2013 N = 16	April 2015 N = 17
Accountability/ Responsibility	**Long Term Perspective/ Vision**	**Ethical/ Integrity**
Ethical/ Integrity	**Accountability/ Responsibility**	Compassion/ Caring
Collaboration/ Teamwork	**Ethical/ Integrity**	**Balance (Home/Work)**
Balance (Home/Work)	**Excellence/ Continuous Improvement**	**Client Satisfaction**
Excellence/ Continuous Improvement	Humor/Fun	**Long Term Perspective/ Vision**
Client Satisfaction	**Balance (Home/Work)**	**Excellence/ Continuous Improvement**
Competence	**Client Satisfaction**	**Accountability/ Responsibility**
Compassion/ Caring	**Collaboration/ Teamwork**	Humor/Fun
Respect	Competence	Results Oriented
Discipline (Long Term Perspective/Vision, Trust/Sincerity)	Discipline	Appreciation Collaboration/Teamwork, Trust/Sincerity, Candor/Honesty/Open tied

Green = Match between top existing and aspirational values in given year.
Bold = Values appearing in all 3 years.

Like Polen and nearly all asset managers, DGI's culture includes the four top values/behaviors in the industry: clients, ethics, collaboration, and excellence. Notice that "compassion/caring" has risen to the number-two spot in the most recent survey. This is a high-performing investment shop with top quartile results, and workers who feel cared for. In the book *Firms of Endearment*, the authors include love as a main reason why FoEs are successful:

It's not possible to fully understand how FoEs outperform their closest competitors without understanding the role of love in their success. FoE executives lead with

strong spines and dedicated resolve, but they retain their capacity to love and inspire
love – in the workplace, in the marketplace and across the full spectrum of their
stakeholder groups.[166]

DGI's leadership team displays the "wisdom and compassion" that defines spiritual intelligence. Fred Martin uses the word love frequently when he talks about the profession and his team. He cares so deeply about the well-being of the industry that he is personally sponsoring a conference, as noted earlier in this book. His intention: Return the industry to its noble calling, especially in the area of fiduciary duty.

Wise and compassionate, Fred is deeply respected by his teammates. His humility allows him to acknowledge his mistakes and apologize quickly. In the investment world, every professional is guaranteed to make many mistakes; it comes with the territory. Leaders who can forgive mistakes, learn from them, and move on build excellent learning cultures. In Fred's own words, he describes his firm's culture this way:

There seem to be four principles without which an organization will not perform to its capability.[167] The first two principles are necessary for an organization to achieve excellent results; the second two are necessary for an organization to achieve superior results.

1) Integrity – Maintaining congruity between what you claim to be and how you act.

2) Responsibility – Holding yourself accountable for successful outcomes.

3) Compassion – Sympathetic concern for the suffering of another, along with the inclination to give aid or support or to show mercy. Compassion is the basis for mutual respect.

4) Forgiveness – The act of renouncing anger or resentment against another person or to absolve from payment of a debt. In a business sense, forgiveness promotes tolerance of others' mistakes and knowledge of our own failings.

If we accept that we must adhere to the above principles in order to maximize our effectiveness as an organization, we can then choose the following six values:

1) Community (Family) – We recognize that each of us is part of several communities, including our families, work associates, and clients. We affirm the importance of maintaining familial relationships within each community. This means we assume [that] these relationships have a permanent place in our lives and we will work very hard to preserve and grow those relationships.

2) Balance – We acknowledge that often there may exist conflicts between various associated communities. For example, there may be a conflict between work and family. We seek to successfully balance the needs of the various communities so as to satisfy our key obligations to each community.

3) Loyalty – We pledge to be faithful, constant, and steadfast to the members of each of the communities to which we each belong.

4) Competency – Even though we are in a competitive industry, we seek to establish our own standards or expectations for our effectiveness. If we meet or exceed our own standards or expectations, our clients will be satisfied and our business will prosper.

5) Proficiency – Proficiency is defined as performing a given skill, art, or branch of learning with correctness and facility. We seek to offer professional investment services to our clients with high proficiency.

6) Learning – Each of us has a life-long commitment to growing in understanding.

The culture survey results from DGI indicate that the firm understands and practices these principles and values.

Another value/behavior that many Focus Elite firms share is "Humor/Fun." The really good firms enjoy working together and realize the positive effect of keeping things light. Our offsites with the senior team at DGI are some of the funniest and most enjoyable that we have. The team constantly kids one another, but it never gets nasty.

On the "passion and purpose" front, DGI is another firm that operates from both. The staff clearly has passion for their work. Also, they have spent several years searching their souls for a strong purpose statement and arrived at the one mentioned earlier:

Enriching lives through long term investing.

They have also adopted the "Firms of Endearment" strategy of embracing the needs of all their stakeholders, not just the owners. Specifically, they have articulated these goals for each stakeholder:

Clients

1. Investment results – rational and impactful
2. Quality relationships/Trusted relationships
3. Fair deal and peace of mind

Employees

1. Meaningful work (mastery and purpose)
2. Appreciation
3. Fair compensation
4. Having fun

Owners

1. Multigenerational spirit of ownership

2. A sustainable franchise

3. 100% employee owned

Not to mislead the reader, Fred and his team are not perfect. They have had their bumps along the way. But they manage to address them, resolve them, and move on with little disruption.

Another Focus Elite team that has Humor/Fun as a core value/behavior is AJO in Philadelphia. For readers who know Ted Aronson, he has a passion for humor – and his culture results indicate that his workers are committed and loyal to the firm and its mission. Culture results for AJO are shown in Figure 10.10.

Figure 10.10 Yearly Comparisons: Existing Culture

April 2010 N = 35	February 2013 N = 48	April 2015 N = 62
Client Satisfaction	Client Satisfaction	Client Satisfaction
Ethical/Integrity	Long Hours/Hard Work	Quality/Precision
Professional	Quality/Precision	Intelligent
Excellence/ Continuous Improvement	Ethical/Integrity	Humor/Fun
Quality/Precision	Humor/Fun	Collaboration/Teamwork
Humor/Fun	Professional	Professional
Intelligent	Analytic/ Research Oriented	Ethical/Integrity
Competence	Hands On/Action Oriented	Long Hours/Hard Work
Candor/Honesty/Open	Excellence/ Continuous Improvement	Competence
Long Hours/Hard Work	Fast Paced Results Oriented tied	Analytic/ Research Oriented

Green = Match between top existing and aspirational values in given year.

AJO, like all the Focus Elite firms, scores well above the industry average on these important success factors, as shown in Figure 10.11.

Figure 10.11 Success Factors

Success Factors (N = 38)	% Agree			% Disagree		
As an organization, we have the ability to attract top talent.	99%	81%	**94%**	0%	10%	**3%**
We are free from silos in our organization.	65%	45%	**50%**	21%	33%	**29%**
We have strong talent management which includes career pathing and succession planning.	76%	48%	**68%**	13%	33%	**17%**
We have and ownership mentality, our employees think like owners of the business.	92%	60%	**78%**	2%	24%	**12%**
We are good at executing plans.	96%	70%	**83%**	0%	15%	**9%**
Our senior team communicates well (clear and transparent).	83%	65%	**82%**	8%	22%	**11%**
We have the resources to do our work well.		98%	78%		0%	16%

Black = The Focus Elite. Blue = Industry.
Agree = slightly agree, agree, strongly agree. Disagree = slightly disagree, disagree, strongly disagree.

Another value that Ted Aronson practices at AJO is generosity. He is a good example of the leadership that Adam Grant describes in his book, *Give and Take*. Grant, a Wharton professor, makes a powerful case for the value of generosity. From his research, Grant found these values associated with givers and takers (Table 10.1)

Table 10.1 Generosity: Takers and Givers

Taker Values	Giver Values
Wealth (money, material possessions)	Helpfulness (working for the well-being of others)
Power (dominance, control over others)	Responsibility (being dependable)
Pleasure (enjoying life)	Social justice (caring for the disadvantaged)
Winning (doing better than others)	Compassion (responding to the needs of others)

Note that the taker values are associated more with self and ego, whereas the giver values are associated more with selflessness and other-orientation. Maslow would place the taker values in the bottom three rungs of his hierarchy, whereas the giver values are more representative of the Higher Self. There is nothing wrong with any of the listed values; they are common to all of us. Who doesn't want more money or occasional pleasures? However, "in the majority of the world's cultures, including that of the United States, the majority of people endorse 'giving' as their single most important guiding principle."[168]

So, why do so many professionals seem to endorse the "taker" side of the values chart? Grant writes, "The fear of being judged as weak or naïve prevents many people from acting like givers at work."[169] Grant explores the pressures that most of us feel in this tug of war between giving and taking:

> People who prefer to give often feel pressured to lean in the taker direction when they perceive the workplace as zero-sum. Whether it's a company with forced ranking systems, a group of companies vying to win the same clients, or a school with required grading curves and more demand than supply for desirable jobs, it's only natural to assume that peers will lean more towards taking than giving. "When they anticipate self-interested behavior from others," explains Stanford psychologist Dale Miller, people feel that they'll be exploited if they operate like givers, so they conclude that "pursuing a competitive orientation is the rational and appropriate thing to do." There's even evidence that just putting on a business suit and analyzing a Harvard Business School case study is enough to significantly reduce the attention that people pay to relationships and the interests of others. The fear of exploitation by takers is so pervasive, writes the Cornell economist Robert Frank, that "by encouraging us to expect the worst in others it brings out the worst in us: dreading the role of the chump, we are often loathe to heed our nobler instincts."

The leaders of the Focus Elite firms demonstrate much more of a giver attitude. Consider another Focus Elite firm, Bridgeway Capital Management, which is clearly of the giver mindset.

This quant firm is living the "Firms of Endearment" model. The subtitle of that book is *How World-Class Companies Profit from Passion and Purpose*. And remember Duncan's claim that investment firms are long on passion but short on purpose. Well, Bridgeway is another firm that is long on both. Part of the firm's mission statement – get ready for this one – is to end genocide on the planet. Yes, this is an INVESTMENT firm! (When I asked the founder, John Montgomery, if they lead with that statement in pitches he smiled and said, "Well, not exactly.") But the firm does give half of its profits to non-profits that address their larger mission; employees, referred to as Partners, not only know the firm's mission but embrace it. Again, because the core desire of our growth needs is to make a positive difference, employees at Bridgeway are only too happy to work for a firm with a deep purpose. By the way, Bridgeway is another *P&I* "Best Places to Work."

Just look at how different the DNA of Bridgeway (Figure 10.12) is from that of the typical investment firm.

Figure 10.12 Top 10 Values – Existing Culture:
Check the values/behaviors that best describe your current culture.
(10 choices, 73 options)

N = 28	Number of Responses	Bridgeway Percent	Industry Percent
Collaboration/Teamwork	16	57%	36%
Ethical/Integrity	15	54%	38%
Community/Social Responsibility	15	54%	9%
Compassion/Caring	15	54%	8%
Analytic/Research Oriented	13	46%	32%
Long-term Perspective/Vision	12	43%	23%
Positive	12	43%	15%
Commitment	10	36%	19%
Generosity (time, talent, resources)	10	36%	7%
Respect	10	36%	19%

Green = Match between top existing and aspirational values. Shaded colors = 20% difference with industry.

Notice that the GREEN boxes on the right are strong statements about the firm's culture. In each case, the firm's commitment to the value/behavior is at least 20% higher than the industry. Which values are we talking about for Bridgeway? These:

• Collaboration/Teamwork

• Community/Social Responsibility

• Compassion/Caring

• Long-Term Perspective/Vision

• Positive

• Generosity (time, talent, resources)

Fascinating. We are looking at a whole new mindset for a successful investment manager. These are bright GREEN and YELLOW values/behaviors. Of course, leadership at Bridgeway demonstrates the YELLOW trait of appreciating all the skills of the different mindsets. Founder John Montgomery is a data hound, who respects numbers, formulas, and big-data (ORANGE, but with strong YELLOW skills). President Tammira Philippe has a Stanford MBA and McKinsey background, so she is no stranger to the ORANGE mindset. In her own words, Tammira describes Bridgeway's success, culture, and journey so far:[170]

> During my 11 years with Bridgeway, I've seen the advantages of our unique company culture and commitment to statistically driven, evidence-based investing. We're building a new model for the investment management industry – one that benefits our clients, our Partners, and our communities. I'm excited to lead Bridgeway and work with our strong team to build an enduring firm that strives for better investment outcomes for our clients and brings positive change to the world.

And if skeptical and practical ORANGE asks, "How are Bridgeway's financial results?," the answer is excellent:

- From 2011–2016, we grew almost four-fold from $2.0 billion to $7.7 billion in assets under management, at a compound annual growth rate of over 30% per year. We have been able to do that through no net new staff, by strategic choices and investing in professional development, technology, and outsourcing.

- Bridgeway is on a rapid growth trajectory – in sharp contrast to industry trends for equity asset managers. We attribute that success to our strong commitment to clients, colleagues, and community that has been the foundation of our remarkable corporate culture since the firm was founded in 1993. Putting investors' interests first is a hallmark of the firm's unique culture and core business values of integrity, performance, efficiency and service. Committed to community impact, Bridgeway donates 50% of its profits to non profit and charitable organizations.

- Much of our growth since 2011 has been through a sub-advised partnership that Bridgeway launched in 2012 to allow us to focus on our passion and core competency in statistically driven, evidence-based investment management.

- Another significant part of our growth since 2011 was a strategic partnership where we collaborated closely on the design of two strategies that could fit into a well-defined asset allocation model. That success was a direct result of extending externally some strong collaboration skills that we have honed and developed internally through our commitment to servant leadership and teamwork.

- Part of our success has been a result of the longevity and stability of the Bridgeway team. When you combine all our investment, trading, and risk management professionals, we have been working together at Bridgeway on average for over a decade. Without a doubt, that is a result of the culture we have built and translates into benefits for our clients as we work to continue to attract and retain the most talented professionals in the business. We do not believe it is by chance that our largest strategy, in terms of assets, has had striking consistency and stability, outperforming its primary benchmark 100% of the time over 3-year rolling periods since inception over a decade ago.

- The road has not always been smooth, however, and our culture contributed tremendously to keeping the firm together through a substantial downturn from 2007–2011. While assets had mostly only gone up from 1993 through 2007, Bridgeway experienced a significant decline in assets from 2007 through 2011, along with many of our peers, due to market and our own underperformance in key strategies. Assets declined from $6.1 billion in 2007 to $2.0 billion at the end of 2011 – a loss of almost 70% at a compound annual loss rate of over 20% per year.

- There were some difficult times, yet we were able to endure and even invest in new professionals to position us for the opportunities we are capturing today. In fact, Bridgeway has only lost one portfolio manager since the inception of the firm in 1993. That does not mean we have not had to make some tough decisions during difficult periods.

- Another aspect of our recent success is that the humility and candor that are embedded in our corporate culture led us to bring in outside experts to substantially improve our investment, communications, and marketing efforts. This enabled us to support our new sub-advisory partner and other existing partners in understanding how we invest better than we had in the past. For now, that looks to have been a missing link that we expect to lead to more success as we aspire to grow in the institutional market going forward.

Some readers at large firms may be wondering whether FCG's experience extends to larger firms. Yes. Although it's more challenging to build a great culture in a larger firm – much like earning alpha in larger portfolios – it is possible. Mawer Investment Management Ltd. has well over 100 employees and offices in three cities: Calgary, Toronto, and Singapore. They've been performing and growing steadily in large part due to excellent leadership and a strong culture. Their tagline, mentioned earlier, is "Be Boring. Make Money™." And they do. Though we would argue that they are not boring, we would also hold them up as a remarkable example of a leadership team that can place the interests of clients first. In fact, they are so committed to clients that they refuse to call any of their team members "sales people." They only think in terms of "client facing." As proof of this claim, FCG can offer up our experience at a recent strategic retreat. Co-author Michael Falk made these comments regarding candor and integrity at the retreat:

It was one of the most candid business dialogues I've ever seen. A group of some 15 partners assembled to discuss the future of their firm which had been remarkably successful but was approaching capacity for some of their mandates.

One-by-one, they shared their personal goals for the next three to five years; everyone had the space and safety to be honest. The sharing included statements about individuals potentially changing their focus or role within the firm, or even potentially retiring. And these statements were made in full view of their colleagues.

Following the dialogue, which was highly curious, with lots of respectful questions, a vote was taken to determine their interest level in pursuing a variety of strategic options – from focusing on current mandates only to fueling growth by adding new investment platforms.

More dialogue ensued, including some strongly held views. The vote was taken and a strong consensus emerged to stay the course with the firm's current strategy – even if it involved closing mandates and limiting future growth. Why? Because they were most concerned with doing the right thing for clients as "stewards of capital," which did not include developing new investment processes or alternative investments. Also, leaders wanted their "younger" employees to have the opportunity to build on what was already in place.

After dinner, a casual discussion took place on sofas around a fireplace, debriefing the earlier meeting and the decision they reached. The conversation was friendly, candid, and humorous. And with full recognition that the strategic decision made earlier may slow the firm's future growth – a consequence that was okay with all the partners.

The mission and values of Mawer are stated as follows:

Mission: To be our clients' most trusted investment manager: a position earned through long term investment excellence, strong client partnerships, and a commitment to always to do the right thing.

Values: "Do the right thing": act with integrity, put clients' interests first, pursue excellence, work as a team, think long term.

Of course, the key question about statements like these is: Are they living these words? FCG's experience with Mawer yields a resounding yes. ORANGE competition and analytical excellence combined with GREEN humanism and service mentality provide a strong platform for Mawer.

Like the other Focus Elite firms, Mawer's culture has been consistently strong for a number of years, as seen in its culture results in Figure 10.13.

Figure 10.13 Yearly Comparisons: Existing Culture

April 2010 N = 54	November 2012 N = 82	May 2015 N = 112
Ethical/Integrity	Client Satisfaction	Client Satisfaction
Excellence/ Continuous Improvement	Excellence/ Continuous Improvement	Ethical/Integrity
Client Satisfaction	Ethical/Integrity	Excellence/ Continuous Improvement
Long term Perspective/ Vision	Long term Perspective/ Vision	Collaboration/Teamwork
Collaboration/Teamwork	Professional	Long term Perspective/ Vision
Professional	Candor/Honesty/Open	Candor/Honesty/Open
Respect	Collaboration/Teamwork	Curious/ Open to new ideas
Candor/Honesty/Open	Accountability/ Responsibility	Professional
Curious/ Open to new ideas	Intelligent	Global (perspective, leadership, etc.)
Accountability/ Responsibility	Curious/ Open to new ideas	Respect

Green = Match between top existing and aspirational values in given year.

Note that the investment "Big 4" are the top values for 2015: clients, integrity, excellence, and teamwork. (Remember that all values shown in GREEN are both "have" and "want" values.) Mawer has developed a remarkably strong culture, which they've been working on consistently for more than a decade. But, like all the Focus Elite firms, Mawer went through a "dark night of the soul" in the early 2000s when the first generation and second generation of leaders were at odds, with the second generation close to leaving. To their credit – and eventual success – Mawer did the hard work of reconciling differences and staying together. Now Mawer is arguably one of the most admired investment firms in Canada, with competitors frequently asking FCG, "What are they doing at Mawer?" In other words, "What is their secret?" Well, largely what we've been describing in this book: good leveraging of BLUE, ORANGE, and GREEN talent, under YELLOW leadership that understands the value of each: all of which results in a superb culture that serves all the stakeholders.

As noted earlier, the culture is client-centric and service-oriented. When asked whether firm leaders are more growth oriented (owner-centric) or performance oriented (client-centric), the answer is strongly for the latter (Figure 10.14).

Figure 10.14 Focus: Asset Gathering vs. Investment Performance

Investment team leaders are mostly focused on asset gathering (sales-centric)

Investment team leaders are mostly focused on fund performance (investment-centric)

AVG: 30%/70%   STANDARD DEVIATION: +/- 22%

Nearly 100%, very strongly 1st statement	1
90%/10%, strongly 1st statement	3
75%/25%, somewhat strongly 1st statement	0
60%/40%, slightly strong 1st statement	4
50%/50%, neutral/balanced	28
40%/60%, slightly strong 2nd statement	9
25%/75%, somewhat strongly 2nd statement	26
10%/90%, strongly 2nd statement	24
Nearly 100%, very strongly 2nd statement	12
?	5

Though intensely competitive in their market performance (ORANGE), the employees see themselves as highly collaborative and highly trusted (GREEN) (Figures 10.15 and 10.16).

FIGURE 10.15 Strategy: Compete World, Collaborate Inside vs. Compete Outside and Inside

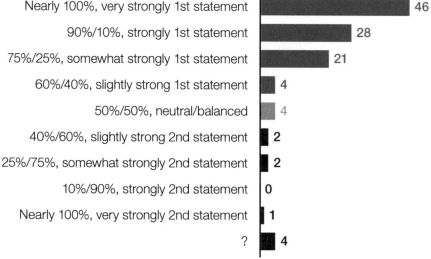

Strategy is "compete with outside world, collaborate internally"

Strategy is "compete outside and inside. Let the cream rise. Every man for himself"

AVG: 86%/14%   STANDARD DEVIATION: 19%

Nearly 100%, very strongly 1st statement	46
90%/10%, strongly 1st statement	28
75%/25%, somewhat strongly 1st statement	21
60%/40%, slightly strong 1st statement	4
50%/50%, neutral/balanced	4
40%/60%, slightly strong 2nd statement	2
25%/75%, somewhat strongly 2nd statement	2
10%/90%, strongly 2nd statement	0
Nearly 100%, very strongly 2nd statement	1
?	4

Figure 10.16 People: Trust vs. Managed

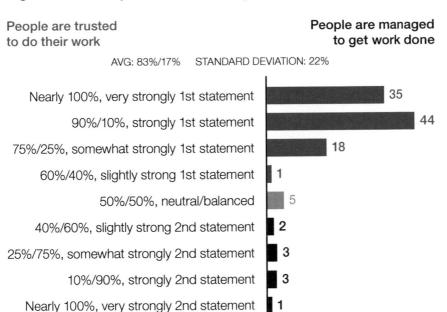

People are trusted
to do their work

**People are managed
to get work done**

AVG: 83%/17%   STANDARD DEVIATION: 22%

Nearly 100%, very strongly 1st statement	35
90%/10%, strongly 1st statement	44
75%/25%, somewhat strongly 1st statement	18
60%/40%, slightly strong 1st statement	1
50%/50%, neutral/balanced	5
40%/60%, slightly strong 2nd statement	2
25%/75%, somewhat strongly 2nd statement	3
10%/90%, strongly 2nd statement	3
Nearly 100%, very strongly 2nd statement	1

Leadership at Mawer believes that the following factors have combined for their success:

- Delivering long-term investment excellence

- Developing strong partnerships with clients

- Continually strengthening the firm's culture

- A commitment to staying independent

Mawer's president, Michael Mezei, summed up his view of the firm's success this way:

I think our success has come from staying focused on a few key things: building and reinforcing our culture; our unwavering commitment to our "Be Boring. Make Money™" investment philosophy and approach; staying close to our clients; and finally, remaining independent – our independence has let us focus on "doing the right thing" for our clients and our firm, without the distraction of answering to others.[171]

There are other examples of excellent investment leadership that is moving beyond bright ORANGE to an integrated approach, appreciating all the strengths of other mindsets. Culture results for these additional Focus Elite firms mirror the ones shown in this chapter. We've included short summaries in Appendix 4, highlighting a noteworthy aspect of each.

These successful firms combine purpose and passion, while integrating the benefits of BLUE, ORANGE, and GREEN with the wisdom of YELLOW in charge.

Let's drill down a little deeper into the heart of the investment engine in these firms. FCG got curious about the factors that explain their investment success; that is, their admirable long-term records. So, we invited investment teams from 10 firms to respond to a survey addressing this question: "Which factors do you believe contribute to your success?" The findings support our view that winning investment firms – and teams – succeed because they skillfully combine ORANGE (the hard side) and GREEN (the soft side).

Summary:

- Some asset managers are emerging as Elite firms that combine the different mindsets to achieve strong cultures and excellent results.

- These firms combine purpose with passion, develop high levels of trust, and rally around a core set of values.

- Like Firms of Endearment, these Elite firms aim to serve all stakeholders, not just shareholders.

- YELLOW is emerging as a leadership style in these firms. These firms are led by people with greater levels of self-awareness and an appreciation for different mindsets.

- There is a generous quality to them that reflects more Higher Self than Ego.

---

[159] On our website: www.focusCgroup.com
[160] https://www.polencapital.com/about-us/
[161] Duncan, *Discovering Phi*, p. 16.
[162] Suzanne Duncan, personal telephone communication, May 8, 2017.
[163] *The Folly of Blame* is available on our website: www.focuscgroup.com
[164] Dan Davidowitz, personal email communication, March 7, 2016.
[165] These mindset designations are determined by a personality assessment called the Enneagram (see Appendix 6). Moss is a "3 Achiever," Davidowitz is a "2 Caretaker," and Ficklin is a "1 Perfectionist." For more on this assessment, visit our website and see the paper *What Kind of Investor Are You?* (2015): http://www.focuscgroup.com/wp-content/uploads/2015/11/what-type-of-investor-are-you.pdf
[166] *Firms of Endearment*, p. 89.

167 These values are described extensively in Doug Lennick & Fred Kiel's book, *Moral Intelligence* (Upper Saddle River, NJ: Wharton School Publishing, 2007). Their research shows that leaders globally tend to recognize these values as core to a good organization.

168 Adam Grant, *Give and Take* (New York: Penguin Books, 2014), p. 21.

169 *Ibid.*

170 Tammira Philippe, personal email communication, January 13, 2017.

171 Michael Mezei, personal email communication, January 11, 2017.

CHAPTER ELEVEN

Investment Teams in the New Era: The Mindsets at Work

Drilling down into the investment teams, we see a strong case for understanding and employing the mindsets we've been discussing in this book. From an investment professional point of view, each of the mindsets has strong skillsets to contribute to an asset management team. Specifically, Table 11.1 collates the strengths of each type.

Table 11.1 Mindsets and Skillsets of Investment Professionals

Mindset	Myers-Briggs/ Temperament (Enneagram Types)	Values	Investment Strengths	Typical Approach to Research or Problem Solving
GREEN	NF Idealist (2, 9)	• Collaboration • Consensus • Trust/Respect	Looks for ways to bring out the best from individuals and the team. Often the "glue" that holds team together.	Use different sources to "feel" your way into the research and decide what should be done.
ORANGE	NTJ Rationalist (3, 5, 8)	• Competition • Drive to win • Decisive	Ability to synthesize ideas to form thesis. Will take appropriate risks. Will push for results. Creative.	Design a process to understand the investment and form an opinion.
BLUE	STJ Guardian (1, 6)	• Fact-driven • Order • Logical process	Careful, step-by-step analysis. Deep research. Respect for process and discipline.	Collect as much data as possible before starting to form a hypothesis.

As we've stated in the book, the YELLOW mindset is ideal for leading an investment team. YELLOW can emerge from any of these "earlier" mindsets as the Higher Self becomes more in charge, taking over from the Ego. Hence, in the New Era, firms will be wise to find and develop talented investment professionals who aspire to lead from the Higher Self. For example, an ORANGE person who becomes more self-aware will still display the ORANGE talents – competitive and decisive – but she will have developed the ability to step back and observe herself and the team. YELLOW allows her to be more comprehensive in her thinking because she remains wise and compassionate in the midst of hectic markets. She will resist the Ego's call to jump into Victim, Villain, or Hero mode and remain calm and effective. Another way to think of the YELLOW mindset is that it remains conscious for decision making, rather than going to autopilot. A really good YELLOW portfolio manager knows how to get the best thinking out of each analyst. Buffett praised this attribute as having the right "temperament."

FCG wanted to learn more about how the best investment teams operate, so we invited a number of teams with excellent, long-term track records to participate in a study. Our goal was to explore what, if any, were the common factors that contributed to their success. We wrote a white paper that summarizes the study and its findings: *Top Performing Equity Teams: The Common Factors They Share.*[172] In this chapter, we'll look at how the mindsets discussed earlier contributed to excellent performance for these teams.

In our research – and field work with teams[173] – we found that the most successful teams valued both relationships (GREEN) and process (BLUE and ORANGE). The model that we use to describe these two components of teamwork is shown in Figure 11.1.

Figure 11.1 Framework

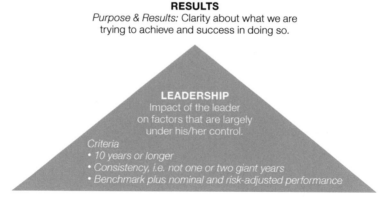

RESULTS
Purpose & Results: Clarity about what we are trying to achieve and success in doing so.

LEADERSHIP
Impact of the leader on factors that are largely under his/her control.

Criteria
- *10 years or longer*
- *Consistency, i.e. not one or two giant years*
- *Benchmark plus nominal and risk-adjusted performance*

RELATIONSHIPS
Relationships & Connection: We respect and trust one another, we enjoy working together, we would choose to work with this team.

PROCESS
Process & Policies: We have clear and repeatable ways that we work together, which includes roles, responsibilities, rules, and decision rights.

Of the 37 factors that we examined in our study, we found that the top 10 factors were evenly distributed between the "soft" (GREEN) factors and the "hard" (BLUE and ORANGE) factors. The factors that seemed to contribute most to winning are shown in Figure 11.2.[174]

Figure 11.2 Success Factors for Top Equity Teams (% agree)

Hard: Process & Structure (% agree)	Soft: Relationships (% agree)
1. Disciplined process (95%)	1. Committed to one another's success (93%)
2. Continuous improvement (94%)	2. Passion for our work (90%)
3. Independence from outside (91%)	3. Enjoy working together (89%)
4. Diversity of thinking styles (86%)	4. Capacity for good debate (86%)
5. Develop our team members (85%)	5. Emotional intelligence (85%)

You can quickly see that the top teams were drawing on the strengths of all the mindsets listed earlier and discussed throughout this book. We were careful to point out in the *Top-Performing Teams* paper that for each of the factors in Figure 11.2 there is a conventional view and what FCG calls "unconventional wisdom." For example, although all teams are expected to have a disciplined process, the unconventional wisdom is that these processes need to be examined over time and continually improved, when warranted. The top teams indicated that they have buy/sell processes. Additionally, there is clarity and acceptance of decision rights: Who is making the final call? What are the ground rules for decision making?

In this way, the top factor on the hard side – disciplined process – overlaps with the second factor: continuous improvement. The best firms are continually reviewing their disciplined process as markets and conditions change. Participant comments indicated that the best teams were comfortable with adhering to the basic philosophy and process while still examining it and updating it. In other words, they did not view upgrades as changing their core process. Rather, the core remains intact, but the way it is implemented could be fine-tuned. BLUE is attracted to process and will push to make sure a good one is in place. ORANGE likes process as well but will push to make sure it is continually questioned and improved. GREEN contributes by finding the value in both views and pushing for respectful debate. One of the best firms commented: "We go off every year on a three-day retreat. We review our process and past decisions in detail. We are always trying to get better."

Another structural aspect of high-performing teams involves the make-up of the team. While the conventional view remains "we can win with smart, hardworking talent," the top teams are aware that cognitive diversity (i.e., different thinking styles) is a competitive advantage. So, the very argument we are proposing in this book – effective use of different mindsets – is supported by the top equity teams. One top team said, "Cognitive diversity is a very important tool in finding a good decision, as it can correct for individual blindspots which might lead to bad judgment."

Indeed, teams that have BLUE, ORANGE, and GREEN mindsets have the advantage over teams that are dominated by just one.

Another "hard" factor that is common to the top teams is development. Often the ORANGE-dominated teams will fall into the bias of overconfidence – ORANGE is naturally self-assured – and dismiss the opportunities for development because "we have investment professionals with CFA designations. We don't need development. We are fully finished products." But when you go back to Chapter 2, and look at the active manager results, you must wonder: How much denial are they in!? The same firms that are underperforming – and there are lots of them – resist development of their analysts! The results from our survey suggest that the best teams do not make this mistake.

Additional support for developing team members comes from a study by Citi Prime Finance.[175] They studied the relationship between development of people and performance at hedge funds and found a significant relationship: Firms that invested in development outperformed firms that did not (Figure 11.3).

Figure 11.3 People Alpha and Returns

Funds that scored in the top half of our people alpha scoring grid out-performed funds in the bottom half.

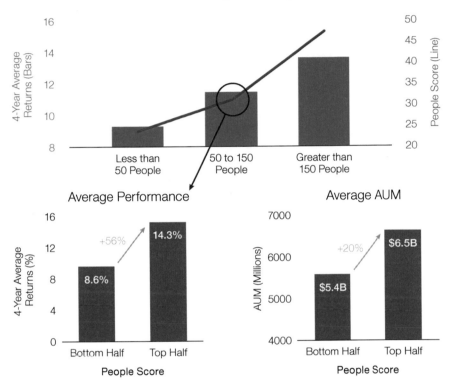

Average Investment Returns & People Scores
for Various Sized Hedge Fund Organizations

- **50 to 150 employee firms** achieved an average 4-year return of 11.4%

- **Hedge funds with 50 to 150 people that scored in the top half** had an average return of 14.3%, a figure that is nearly 600 basis points higher

- **Hedge funds with 50 to 150 people in the bottom half:** average 4-year return of 8.6%

- **The average AUM of the firms:**
    - **Top half:** significantly higher at $6.5 billion
    - **Bottom half:** $5.4 billion average

Turning to the soft side of the commonalities, FCG was reassured to see that these factors matter deeply to the best-performing teams. When Jim attended University of Chicago Business School in the late 70s, there were *no* classes on these skills. None. Nada. And there was no behavioral finance. Richard Thaler would never have been hired as a full professor back then. The thinking has changed greatly in the ensuing decades. Good! Now there is a greater appreciation for the leadership and team dynamics on an investment team. Still, the conventional view remains that investment professionals are competitive and individualistic by nature (ORANGE), so getting them to work well together (GREEN) – to "see themselves as a team" – is an ambitious goal. FCG has been hired by many global investment firms to promote synergy among the different strategies: get the equity folks talking to the fixed income teams, and get the global people talking to the domestic ones. Indeed, in FCG's experience, this is a tough challenge. One CIO told us flat out: "We've tried that several times, including throwing money at it, and never succeeded. So, we've given up. Let them work individually."[176] So, perhaps one of the biggest advantages of top teams is their mindset of being one, unified team whose members have each other's backs. While the conventional view may be that an equity team can win with individual contributors, the unconventional wisdom is: "We are committed to one another's success." One top team commented:

> *Our process and our success is built upon the team and its commitment to each other. Without that commitment, I don't think we'd have the culture of trust which allows us to be creative, make mistakes, and still show up deeply excited to be there the next day.*

In FCG's experience, we have seen many cases where the conventional view is accurate. So, our view is that hiring the right people – the ones who are naturally team players – is the most effective way to achieve this important factor. To this add YELLOW leadership that genuinely appreciates the skillsets of each mindset.

Another important soft factor is "enjoy working together." Again, the conventional view is that liking your team members is a nice-to-have but not a need-to-have. We have heard bright ORANGE PMs say, "I don't really care if my team members like each other; I care if they perform." But the top teams state emphatically that positive rapport is important to top performance (GREEN). Many comments from responders mirrored the following quote:

If we didn't like working with each other, or for the firm, we would be hard-pressed to contribute – over the course of years – the deep creativity necessary to our success.

Finally, top teams understand the importance of emotional intelligence. The term "emotional intelligence" (EQ) was coined by Daniel Goleman and consists of four skillsets, shown in the diagram in Figure 11.4.

Figure 11.4 Emotional Intelligence: Skillsets

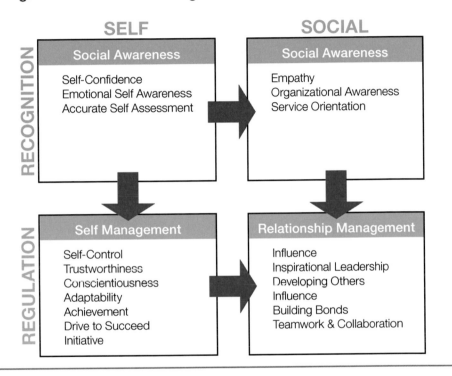

Emotionally intelligent teams are far more productive than teams on "auto-pilot." Research on EQ yields the results shown in Figure 11.5.

Figure 11.5 Benefits of high EQ

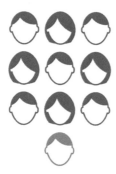

90%
of top
performers
have high EQ

EQ is
responsible for
58%
of your
job performance

People with
high EQ make
$29,000
more annually
than their low
EQ counterparts

Comments from our elite teams were:

- "We recognize this is a very fickle business and that mistakes are made. Therefore, there is a certain level of ego and confidence that is mandatory, but it is also extremely important to be able to admit what you don't know, encourage others, and learn from the inevitable mistakes."

- "In a collaborative environment, we need people to feel safe evaluating each other's ideas. We could do a better job of speaking fairly and considerately, to spur honest feedback."

- "We need to be able to rigorously challenge an idea and the work that went into it, and still walk away from the table as colleagues and friends. That is not easy, and it takes a lot of emotional intelligence in terms of how you conduct yourself in a debate, and how you manage your emotions before and after."

- "Our team is highly emotionally intelligent and collaborative."

- "I do think our culture and our team is a huge intangible asset to our success."

- "Team culture and dynamics is a key consideration for every hire within the firm."

- "I suspect compared with peers, we have more 'emotional intelligence' than 'discipline.' Emotional intelligence is more difficult to develop as it needs a well-aligned, well-performing and stable team environment and it takes time."

The conventional ORANGE view still seems to be that EQ is "nice to have" but not necessary. The key to winning is smart, hard-working people who can leave their emotions at the door. People with high EQ realize that we can't divorce ourselves from our emotions, so it is much better to become self-aware and skillful around emotions than to pretend that we don't have them.[177] The *P&I* "Best Places" firms are all beginning to acknowledge and practice EQ as an important skill for success.

So, these are the top 10 factors – hard and soft – identified by our top teams. FCG can appreciate the wisdom of each, and the danger of adopting the conventional view. We are grateful to the teams that allowed us to survey and study their practices to learn more about their success.

Active managers face a tougher challenge. By some measures, only a handful of teams are delivering on the promise of value-add returns. This chapter has argued that active managers can and do win even in these tough markets, but only by building a great team with BLUE, ORANGE, and GREEN properly integrated. A YELLOW team leader must be adept at both the closed fist (giving clear directions for structural and process factors) and the open hand (creating team dynamics that include trust, safety, open debate, and continuous improvement). The conventional views presented in this chapter represent the path to mediocrity. For teams to truly excel, they must remove their blinders and take a hard look at the reality of their processes and team. Both hard and soft factors matter. The good news is: Teams made up of mortal humans are outperforming. So, it is possible. The bad news is: It is not easy. Teams must move beyond their self-deception and take a hard look at their team members and processes.

Summary:

- Research by FCG on top equity teams reveals common factors that are both "hard" (BLUE and ORANGE mindsets) and "soft" (GREEN mindset).

- YELLOW leadership is extremely important in identifying, valuing, and leveraging the different mindsets.

- Hard skills include factors like discipline, continuous improvement and development.

- Soft skills include factors such as commitment, enjoyment working together, and emotional intelligence (EQ).

- Active management has become a tougher challenge. Conventional approaches will not work in the New Era. Successful investment teams will understand the unconventional wisdom discussed in this chapter and put it to use.

Figure 11.6 The 37 factors, ranked by importance

1. We are disciplined.
2. We have found ways to continually improve, never settling for "good enough."
3. The team is committed to each other and successes.
4. We are independent of outside influencers, i.e. parent company, etc.
5. We have passion for the work, we love it.
6. We enjoy working with each other.
7. We have different thinking styles on our team.
8. The members of our investment team debate well.
9. We develop our team members.
10. As a team, we have "emotional intelligence".
11. We make use of a sizing discipline.
12. We have good working relationships with client service.
13. We are creative.
14. We close strategies, that is, limit AUM growth.
15. Our team has clear decision rights which contribute to our success.
16. We have psychological safety on our team.
17. We have bench strength.
18. We keep journals of our decisions, so we can accurately review our thought processes.
19. We use quantitative tools.
20. We make better use of the information/research we have than our competitors.
21. We believe all team members are working in their "genius", i.e. highest and best use.
22. We do deeper research than others.
23. For our investment decisions, we have an insight differentiated from consensus and validated beyond company management.
24. We make good use of our meeting time.
25. We use a filter to narrow our potential buy list.
26. We make use of a sell discipline.
27. We test and review our filter over time.
28. Our research focuses on a handful of critical factors (or investment controversies) for a given investment.

29. We conduct post-mortems on positions we exit to learn from our experience.

30. We understand the succession plan for our leaders.

31. We have a long-term perspective; a holding period goal of 5+ years.

32. All investment decisions are known by the team before being executed.

33. We have feedback loops to learn how our processes are doing.

34. We have "dedicated research teams" (vs. centralized research).

35. Most, if not all, of our team members have a meaningful amount of money invested in our fund(s).

36. We set price targets.

37. We have one or more stars that drive our success.

---

172 http://www.focuscgroup.com/wp-content/uploads/2015/11/Top-Performing-Equity-Teams.pdf

173 Michael Falk on FCG's team embeds with investment teams for days at a time to learn deeply and advise on their processes.

174 Percentages in the chart indicate the number of participants who agreed that the given factor was crucial to success.

175 Exploring the Concept and Characteristics of "People Alpha" (October 2013); http://www.focuscgroup.com/wp-content/uploads/2015/11/People_Alpha.pdf

176 Name withheld by request.

177 Michael Falk quote, "Neuroscience research shows that emotions are needed to make decisions, and investing is all about decisions."

CHAPTER TWELVE

A Brave New World: From "Value" Investing
to "Values" Investing

Now let's turn to the emergence of GREEN and YELLOW and see how they are changing the landscape of investing. As we explore these new directions, remember that it is vitally important for all participants to embrace and practice their fiduciary duties. If we are ever to rebuild trust in our industry, all mindsets must be vigilant on this front, as discussed in Chapter 8.

First, let's remind ourselves of what the ORANGE world looks like. To the ORANGE investor, success looks like consistent, superior returns. Legendary investors like Buffett, Lynch, and Soros achieved "Hall of Fame" status by posting great numbers over long periods of time. We are not suggesting that great ORANGE investors revise their investment processes: If it ain't broke, don't fix it. They may, however, need to lead their firms differently to attract and retain talent in the New Era, but that topic has been covered in other chapters. From a strictly performance-related view, ORANGE firms that create alpha are doing exactly what they should be doing, assuming they are adhering to legal and fiduciary guidelines. In this chapter, we'll explore the goal of investments from a broader perspective of the GREEN and YELLOW mindsets.

Some with deeply ORANGE mindsets find it hard to wrap their heads around a GREEN perspective concerning the goal of investing. *Shouldn't investing always be about getting the best return for a given level of risk? Isn't "more" always better?* To GREEN, the answer is often "No." GREEN looks at money from this viewpoint: how do I use money to create a happier life and a better world? Not simply, how do I get more of it? In her book, *The Soul of Money*, Lynne Twist takes a very GREEN/YELLOW view of money. She writes about a healthy relationship to money, in which we are in charge of it, and not the other way around. In Twist's words, "a world where the love of money is replaced by the use of money as an expression of love."[178] She challenges three money myths that are dominant in the Western world (ORANGE mindset):

1. "There is not enough." With this fearful mindset, we fight to get our fair share and we rationalize that it's okay when some get less because "there is not enough."

2. "More is always better." Scarcity fears drive us to grow at any cost, with no sense of "enough." Even those with plenty are trapped on the hamster wheel chasing more.

3. "It's always been this way." There is no questioning the status quo despite evolving mindsets. Therefore, the first two statements live on because "they're just reality." (Useful to remember that 200 years ago, women and minorities were inferior and that was "just reality.")

In a very GREEN/YELLOW mindset, Twist challenges us to question the validity of these ORANGE myths:

I challenge you to use the money that flows through your life – and it does flow through all of our lives – to express truth and sufficiency (i.e., having enough).

I challenge you to move the resources that flow through your life toward your highest commitments and ideals, those things you stand for.

I challenge you to hold money as a common trust that we're all responsible for using in ways that nurture and empower us, and all life, our planet, and all future generations.

I challenge you to imbue your money with soul – your soul – and let it stand for who you are, your love, your heart, your word, and your humanity.[179]

This mindset is radically different from the traditional ORANGE mindset, which values winning, growth, and higher returns. The YELLOW mindset embraces both ORANGE and GREEN. Each one is valuable – and the investment world is moving in this broader direction. Sallie Krawcheck founded Ellevest because she "realized the investing industry has been, frankly, 'by men, for men' – and has historically kept women from achieving their financial goals. Sallie has made it her life's mission to unleash women's financial power and get them invested in their biggest goals. Partnering with tech entrepreneur Charlie Kroll, she's assembled a diverse team from product, engineering, design and finance backgrounds.[180] So, if a person feels compelled to take a stand for women in the workplace, they can express that value by investing in the Ellevest funds.

The following is a list of possible fund strategies that would be based on "values" investing as opposed to the traditional risk/return tradeoff. Note that all the points made in Chapter 8 about fiduciary responsibilities would still be front and center for any of these strategies. New strategies in no way excuse or release firms from fiduciary duties.

- **ESG funds.** This strategy is off and running. An estimated "one-fifth of all investment under professional management"[181] in the United States is under the heading of sustainable, responsible, and impact investing. Firms like Boston Common are exclusively devoted to investing in this fashion and are growing and prosperous. They are both ORANGE and GREEN in their approach. Although this approach is still in its infancy, a recent paper states that ESG funds "outperformed the MSCI World Index over the periods February 2007-March 2015 and February 2008-March 2015."[182]

- **Impact investing.** Impact investing refers to investments "made into companies, organizations, and funds with the intention to generate a measurable, beneficial social or environmental impact alongside a financial return."[183]

- **Gender funds.** Ellevest is one example. Eve Ellis at Morgan Stanley runs another gender-based fund. Interestingly, State Street Global Advisors is calling on the more than 3,500 companies it invests in on behalf of its clients to increase gender diversity on their corporate boards.[184]

- **Firms of Endearment.** These funds would hold companies that fit the description from the book discussed earlier. There is an investment firm, Concinnity, that is up and running with this approach. "The premise that a multi-stakeholder operating system (MsOS) is good for companies, good for capitalism and good for investors is not new. A steady and increasing body of work by researchers, corporate authors, academic authors and management consultants has presented compelling arguments for why companies should adopt a multi-stakeholder operating system. But most notably, societal and marketplace expectations about the companies we buy from, work for, invest in and that operate in our communities, are making the adoption of a multi-stakeholder mindset less of an option. The thesis underpinning investment products based on our research is that a multi-stakeholder operating system is well aligned with today's marketplace realities and companies truly committed to it are more likely to thrive."[185]

- **Leadership Capital Index.** Dave Ulrich, professor and author on leadership, has devised an index to measure the strength of leadership in a firm. So, investors who are convinced that better leadership makes for better returns could buy this portfolio. People who are convinced that "when leadership improves, everybody wins" (as Bill Hybels, pastor and author on leadership, believes) could invest in these firms based on their values. Here is how Ulrich describes his work: "My new book, *Leadership Capital Index*, draws on a useful metaphor for how to include, conceive, and audit leadership in the assessment of firm value. A leadership capital index is like a financial confidence index – Moody's or Standard & Poor's. It offers a more thorough way to assess leadership. Most acknowledge that leaders affect an organization's value, but they use simplistic and intuitive approaches to apply that insight. A leadership ratings index would have two dimensions – individual and organizational. Individual refers to the personal qualities (competencies, traits, characteristics) of the key leaders in the organization. Organization refers to the systems (often called human capital) these leaders create to manage leadership throughout the organization and the application of organization systems to specific business conditions."[186]

- **Religious beliefs.** Many portfolios are constructed around the religious beliefs of a certain faith: for instance, Catholic portfolios that support their views, or Muslim portfolios that honor Sharia law.

You get the idea: investing based on a purpose or value, rather than the narrow goal of risk/return. Note that the argument for these funds is not that they consistently outperform traditional funds, but that they may offer competitive returns and do offer psychological and societal benefits of investing in line with one's values. We can imagine dozens of different portfolios based on this premise, because there are dozens of causes in the world. Additional ideas for portfolios constructed on "values" might include:

- **Diversity.** Companies that have distinguished themselves by having built a significantly diverse workforce.

- **Engagement.** Gallup has developed the "Gallup 12" survey for measuring a firm's engagement level.

- **Healthy cultures.** McKinsey has developed a "healthy culture" metric, used by many firms to analyze the level of healthy functioning within their culture.

- **Animal welfare.** Jim's wife is an animal lover and on many occasions has said, "if you find me a fund that supports animal welfare, I'll invest even if I get a lower return!"

- **Spirituality.** Author/consultant Cindy Wigglesworth, discussed earlier, has written a book and designed a metric for measuring the spiritual intelligence (like EQ for emotions). She describes the model in this way:

[T]he SQ21 model translates the most-admired qualities of our spiritual heroes – people like Nelson Mandela, Saint Teresa, or Martin Luther King Jr. – into a set of 21 skills that can be measured and intentionally developed. You will learn how to: Recognize the voice of Higher Self. Live a life that is on-purpose and values-driven. Understand people with very different points of view. Sustain faith during challenging times. Make compassionate and wise decisions, incorporating the best of contemporary and traditional spiritual wisdom in language that is faith neutral and faith-friendly. SQ21 is an invaluable tool for leaders, educators, coaches, consultants and anyone else seeking an effective, rational, and holistic way to embrace spirituality and see results.[187]

For investors who are attracted to this idea of investing in alignment with their values, they could design their own portfolios using Motif Investing's offering. Motif Investing allows you to design your own ETF. With regard to aligning values with investing, founder Hardeep Walia stated the results of a recent survey as follows:

> When Motif asked if respondents would change their investments if they were not aligned with their personal values, 68 percent said yes. Almost three-fifths of the respondents, 57 percent, answered that they would be angry or extremely angry if they found that their investments were misaligned with their personal values.

> We saw an opportunity to give people more complete transparency and give them the information they need to make sure that what's in their portfolios is aligned with their values."[188]

Note that one of our elite CEOs (from the Focus Elite firms) reacted strongly to this chapter, arguing that the fiduciary standard has been violated many times and the industry must focus on adhering to it. Introducing a whole new type of investing – social values investing – may further weaken fiduciary behavior. He was especially critical of clients who asked him and his team to include social values, like E (environment), S (social), or G (governance), into his firm's investment process. Tampering with his process may jeopardize the excellent performance that they've produced over the years. FCG is in complete agreement with this point. We would not advocate changing a successful, alpha-producing strategy to meet client requests for social causes. In fact, that's our whole point: let the two types of investing exist separately, offering choice to investors. If you want ORANGE alpha, then fine. Go to a time-tested producer of alpha and get it. If you want to support women in the workforce (GREEN), then go to a reputable gender fund and invest in it. Now, here's the key to the first point about fiduciary standards: both types of funds must adhere to the fiduciary standard of putting the client first. Arguing that we should limit consumer choice to just the ORANGE alpha funds seems to go against the very grain of free markets and capitalism. Instead, allow the new forms of values investing to arise and flourish but – as an industry – do a better job of promoting and enforcing fiduciary standards for *all* of them.

The point of this chapter was to play with idea of wresting the investment function away from the purely profit-motivated ORANGE and see what happens when RED, BLUE, GREEN, or YELLOW mindsets weigh in with their values. The possibilities are significant for increased happiness on the part of investors, as they find more meaning and purpose in their investments. To use an analogy, imagine asking mature persons how they evaluate their lives (which Clayton Christensen does in his book, *How Will You Measure Your Life?*).[189] We would be surprised to hear anyone say, in Scrooge-like fashion, "My life has been great. I made a ton of money. I'm wealthy as hell! Of course,

I'm divorced three times, and my kids from all the marriages hate me, but who cares? My financial balance sheet is great!" We don't evaluate our lives on the narrow metric of money, so why should we evaluate our investments in this narrow way? If our investment returns are basically going to match the indexes over time – which is what Ellis, Bogle, Swedroe, and others are telling us – then, hey, we'd like to get some satisfaction beyond financial. Namely, by putting our money to work in ways that we think are meaningful. It would be wonderful, in our view, if investment advisors started their interviews with clients by asking, "What are your core values, and what is meaningful to you? Can we align your investments with them and still harness the power of compounding?"

Summary:

- Traditional ORANGE investing has focused on superior returns for a given level of risk.

- GREEN investing would broaden the concept of investing to include aligning one's values with the investments in one's portfolio.

- Investors could choose to seek the highest return possible (ORANGE) or to align their investments with their values (GREEN) and still pursue a competitive return.

- ESG and other forms of values investing are emerging rapidly.

- The fiduciary standard would still prevail for all approaches, both traditional and new.

---

[178] Lynne Twist, *The Soul of Money* (New York: W.W. Norton, 2006), p. 247.

[179] Ibid., p. 257.

[180] https://www.ellevest.com/our_story

[181] The Forum for Sustainable and Responsible Investment, "Report on US SRI Investing Trends 2016," p. 5; http://www.ussif.org/files/SIF_Trends_16_Executive_Summary(1).pdf

[182] Herb Blank, Gregg Sgambati, & Zack Truelson, "Best Practices in ESG Funds," *The Journal of Investing* 25(2), (Summer 2016).

[183] https://en.wikipedia.org/wiki/Impact_investing

[184] Meaghan Kilroy, "SSGA Sends Out Edict for Companies to Increase Gender Diversity on Boards," *P&I* (March 7, 2017); http://www.pionline.com/article/20170307/ONLINE/170309872/ssga-sends-out-edict-for-companies-to-increase-gender-diversity-on-boards?newsletter=editors-picks&issue=20170307#utm_medium=email&utm_source=newsletters&utm_campaign=pi-editors-picks-20170313cci_r=30488

[185] http://www.concinnityadvisors.com/investment-theme

[186] Dave Ulrich, "Introducing the Leadership Capital Index—Intersection of Human Capital and Investors," March 31, 2015; https://www.td.org/Publications/Blogs/Human-Capital-Blog/2015/03/Introducing-the-Leadership-Capital-Index

[187] Cindy Wigglesworth of Deep Change, https://www.deepchange.com/about/meet_us

[188] *Financial Advisor (FA)*, March 8, 2017; http://www.fa-mag.com/news/it-s-not-a-robo—motif-launches-custom-automated-impact-investing-31734.html?section=3&page=2

[189] Clayton Christensen, *How Will You Measure Your Life?* (2012); http://www.measureyourlife.com/

CHAPTER THIRTEEN

Client Facing: Financial Advisors and Consultants

I ntermediaries can play a vital role in the investment world. Charley Ellis and Suzanne Duncan both suggest in their writings that the investment world could better serve the population at large if more of its brainpower and talent were funneled into the important role of the financial advisor or consultant. Specifically, the 60% of the industry's resources that were expended in finding alpha could be repositioned to help citizens approach their finances in a responsible and thoughtful fashion. As discussed in Chapter 12, that could start with a more holistic approach to investing. Ellis states in *Index Revolution* that investment professionals should concern themselves with helping clients articulate their core values, their true financial goals, and how they can achieve them. Ellis writes:

The curse of active investing is not simply that it reduces returns, which it usually does, but that, with so much complexity, it diverts our attention from the profoundly important long-term investment policy decisions on which all investors should concentrate their time, energy, and thought.

Each investor is unique. That's why it is important that indexing enables each of us to concentrate on our core values and your personal long-term investment objectives. Investors who accept the challenge and the opportunity will shift their emphasis from reliance on the day-to-day craft of active investing and turn to the professional service of investment counseling – and shift from almost inevitably losing a little here and a little there to assured long-term winning.

Active investing can be interesting and exciting, but we all owe it to ourselves to remember that investing is not just a recreational game, it is serious business. Fortunately, there is another kind of serious "game" in investing, a game we ALL can win because victory doesn't depend (like boxing) on beating others, but (like golf) on mastering ourselves.[190]

Ellis raises several important points here. First, the shift from active to passive: The industry has sold the unrealistic and self-serving idea to the public that it's possible to "win" big in the markets through active investing. For example, a neighbor approached Jim recently and said, "Hey, Jim, you know about investing and markets and that kind of stuff. We've just sold our business and come into some money. What do the smart people do with their money?" The suggestion from this neighbor is that there are two tiers of investing: ordinary folks, who represent "dumb" money and make paltry returns; and the "smart" money that invests and makes big bucks. Jim did his best to assure this neighbor that there isn't a secret sauce that allows some people to make big returns, while others flounder. This notion allowed Bernie Madoff to sell his unrealistic performance story to all-too-willing investors. The reality is that only a few active managers will win, and it is very difficult to know in advance who they will be. (Again, FCG is not arguing that investors should eliminate active funds altogether.) Jim told this neighbor that he should talk to a few of the financial advisors that FCG knows and respects and see what makes sense for a long-term strategy.

Second, financial advisors, as Ellis clearly states, should help clients think through and articulate their goals and then establish a sensible long-term approach. Advisors should help clients understand their role in the investment process – core values, goals, objectives, aligning couples on the aforementioned, and staying-the-course – and *not* expect clients to have an interest in or understanding of market mechanics. As shown earlier in this book, too many advisor newsletters are filled with market minutiae in which the typical client has little interest. Nor should they, necessarily. A Toyota dealership does not expect you to know how engines run or anti-lock brakes operate. You simply want to know things like: Is the car reliable? Will it get me from point A to point B? How often do I need to change the oil? What are the safety features on the car? How much does it cost to buy and maintain? The proper discussion with a financial advisor should be about *outcomes*. Once agreed on outcomes, then the advisors' job is to make it happen through their expert knowledge of planning techniques and products.

Third, Ellis stresses the win/win attitude for advisors and clients, rather than the win/lose scenario. We're surprised that so many advisory firms still put performance front and center in their client-facing meetings. As Ellis stated in the preceding quote, each client is unique. The proper discussion is: Are we on track for the goals that we discussed, some of which may be social? If you train clients to play the performance game, then that's what they will do. They will open their report to the page with performance, quickly assess whether you've beaten the benchmark, and decide whether or not to fire you. That's the wrong discussion.

A more important role for investment advisors is to help clients with the psychological aspects of investment. Advisors need to be the calm, reassuring voice in the midst of financial market nonsense. Picture Jim Cramer shouting and waving his arms wildly as he describes today's market action. Can you be the voice of sanity that helps clients ignore that nonsense and leave your office with a calm sense of "we are on track for the goals we've established"?

A relevant question, based on Ellis's points, is this: Are financial advisors and analysts, on average, equipped to make this change? That is, are they equipped to help clients manage emotional and behavioral challenges? FCG has some doubts. A larger portion of their training should be emotional intelligence (so-called EQ), which targets self-awareness and self-management. Money is an emotion-laden topic for all of us. For some it represents status, for others power, still others see it as a measure of winning. The emotionally savvy advisor – or financial-analyst-turned-advisor – could be hugely helpful in understanding clients' underlying motives and helping them achieve clarity and sanity around investment goals – and attain the temperament to carry out the plan. (Remember, Buffett is known for his comment that temperament (EQ) is more important than IQ in successful investing.) If you feel that your EQ is low, don't despair: there is a clear curriculum of skills that are learnable for anyone interested.[191]

Our culture is a bit nutty on the whole topic of money. Again, we tend to think that in order to be happy, it helps to be wealthy. Advisors, starting with themselves, could be a powerful force in society for providing education and perspective around financial sanity. Again, in Lynne Twist's book, *The Soul of Money*, which we think should be required reading for all financial advisors, she offers this advice:

> *The Soul of Money offers a way to realign our relationship with money to be more truthful, free, and potent, enabling us to live a life of integrity and full self-expression that is consistent with our deepest core values, no matter what our financial circumstances. This book is not about turning away from money or simplifying our expenditures, or doing budgets or financial planning, although wisdom gained will be relevant to all those activities. This book is about living consciously, fully and joyfully in our relationship with money, and learning to understand and embrace its flow. It is about using the unexamined portal of our relationship with money to deliver a widespread transformation in all aspects of our lives.[192]*

Twist describes the very same dichotomy that we've examined in the Maslow hierarchy: the growth needs (Twist calls this "soul") that lead to joy, and the deficiency needs (Ego) that create fear.

Each of us experiences a lifelong tug-of-war between our money interests [deficiency needs] and the calling of our soul [growth needs]. When we're in the domain of soul, we act with integrity. We are thoughtful and generous, allowing, courageous, and committed. We recognize the value of love and friendship. We admire a small thing well done. We experience moments of awe in the presence of nature and its unrefined beauty. We are open, vulnerable, and heartful. We have the capacity to be moved, and generosity is natural. We are trustworthy and trusting of others, and our self-expression flourishes. We feel at peace with ourselves and confident that we are an integral part of a larger, more universal experience, something greater than ourselves. [In FCG's work with clients, we call this mindset "over the line." It is characterized by the Higher Self, which is free of fear and operates from good intentions and trust.]

When we enter the domain of money, there often seems to be a disconnect from the soulful person we have known ourselves to be. [FCG sees this all the time in compensation engagements, as if the normally mature, thoughtful, and trustworthy professionals become possessed by the "dark" side.] It is as if we are suddenly transported to a different playing field where all the rules have changed. In the grip of money, those wonderful qualities of soul seem to be less available. We become smaller. We scramble or race to "get what's ours." We often grow selfish, greedy, petty, fearful, or controlling, or sometimes confused, conflicted, or guilty. We see ourselves as winners or losers, powerful or helpless, and we let those labels deeply define us in ways that are inaccurate, as if financial wealth and control indicate innate superiority, and lack of them suggest a lack of worth or basic human potential. Visions of possibility dissolve. We become wary and mistrusting, protective of our little piece, or helpless and hopeless. We sometimes feel driven to behave in ways inconsistent with our core values, and unable to act differently.[193] [FCG calls this mindset "under the line." It is characterized by drama, high emotionality, and defensiveness. Rarely do discussions from below the line have a constructive outcome.]

FCG worked with a financial advisor where the CEO of the firm was "unable to act differently." He is a good man, with a good heart, but he was completely in the grip of his deficiency needs. Life experiences, personal and professional, had caused him to believe that "everyone is out for himself" and "you can't trust people." Our work with this firm involved succession – for the CEO – and compensation for all the partners. You can imagine how difficult the negotiations were as long as the CEO operated from this mindset! Our advice to him was: In order to gain trust, you must give trust. But, because this CEO was quite convinced of his view that people in general and his partners specifically were selfish and untrustworthy, little progress was made. All during this engagement, we kept asking ourselves, "Is this the right person to be meeting with clients and counseling them on their finances?" When he himself is caught in the "grip of money" as Twist describes? How can this CEO help clients become sane around money, when he's acting insane?! How can he encourage good financial behaviors, like calmness, trust, and patience?

Financial advisors in the New Era should be self-aware about their own relationship to money, so that they can help clients become savvy and "over the line." Advisors should have worked through their own money issues so that they truly are at peace with themselves and can counsel clients from that viewpoint.

One financial advisor who is redefining the investment experience is Lawrence Ford, CEO/Founder and Whole Advisor™ at Conscious Capital Wealth Management (CCWM). Dubbed "The Shaman of Wall Street" by the *Washington Post*, Ford has dedicated much of his life to being a bridge between the modern world of business/finance and the ancient world of wisdom. Here is a bit of Ford's story:

In 1989 – just a couple years out of college – Founder and CEO Lawrence Ford decided he wanted to help make the world a better place. As he looked around, it appeared that money was controlling people. He thought it should be the other way around. Never a follower of convention, Ford decided the only authentic way to follow his purpose was to start his own financial advisory practice. Just five short years later, and lots of macaroni and cheese dinners, he made it to the top of the charts with unprecedented rapid growth in clients.

At age 30, he stood backstage as one of the top ten advisors in the nation at a National Leaders Conference in Banff, Canada, and was about to be paraded in front of 2,500 other top advisors. He stood alone as the other nine advisors backstage with him mingled among themselves. The group finally made it over to where Ford was standing and asked, "Hey kid, tell us what your secret is – how did you make it here so fast?" Ford responded in his natural, authentic way and shared, "There's no secret – we just love every single client." They all walked away. That is when Ford realized that he was a zebra in a herd of horses.

After a decade of esteemed accomplishments in and out of the business world, Ford decided to be a catalyst for change – impacting the investment advisory model that has not kept up with the generations and needs of the individuals in our midst; hence what has developed is the model for the future of the advisory practice and interaction with people and their life choices.

Part of this process is through a hybrid relationship that empowers the client interaction through the use of state-of-the art technology which enables the dialogue between advisor and client in a virtual and non-threatening environment while providing the same intimacy as an in-person meeting. Bringing the best of all worlds together, the holistic, "robo-advisor" and traditional face-to-face meetings. In addition, inclusive in the overall relationships are coaches that focus on life planning, life transition, personal fitness and nutrition which are performed virtually except of course for the massage therapist that resides in the LiveWhole® centers.[194]

Ford's perspective is to awaken clients going through transition to the power of money and how to use money to make the world a better place. "Money is just a tool," Ford notes. "It helps people achieve true wealth, [but] beyond meeting basic needs, money is 'useless.' Money is there to power our dreams and passions; to fuel us, but not rule us." Ford continued: "As we work with clients, we look to build more than just money, it is about understanding and developing dreams, wellness and a person's whole life." The firm is revolutionizing the industry with its whole approach to investing, which focuses not only on building wealth, but also on supporting all aspects of a person's life and wellbeing. "At Conscious Capital Wealth Management, we are different from the ordinary financial advisory experience."[195]

Ford describes the firm's mission as "using the power of money to make the world a better place – helping clients live their dreams." In short, Ford helps clients achieve financial peace of mind. Contrast this approach with the typical financial advisor who is focused narrowly on beating a benchmark and gathering more "share of wallet."

In the phone call with Ford, he said that his office services include a masseuse and a therapist. He added that many clients, when they see CCWM's full offering, break into tears, saying, "I never knew a service like this was available." The strong reaction from these clients indicates the deep need from people everywhere to bridge the gap that Twist described earlier: between our Higher Self (soul) and our everyday needs, which depend on money. We all want a wise person to help us find peace and happiness in this regard – and the bright ORANGE mindset is not wired to give us that wisdom. We need people who have moved up the Maslow hierarchy, into the YELLOW mindset, and have achieved their own peace in their relationship with money. "We are a movement, not just a business," Ford adds. "It's awakening people to the reality around them and moving them into their own power and realizing the totality of who they are."

The crucial role of the financial advisor offers an important value-add. They can be the "money therapists" who help people establish a healthy and sane relationship to money. First, though, financial advisors must develop their own healthy relationship to money. Only then they can advise clients on what is involved in achieving it for themselves. For many investment professionals, the only honest approach is the 12-step one: "My name is so-and-so, and I'm recovering from my own money issues."

A large proportion of the industry is excessively driven by money. Instead of being supremely happy that they are 1%ers doing fascinating work, they instead lose sleep over "only" making X million dollars. (During the writing of this chapter, Jim met with a PM who is "only making" $14 million per year. He and his CEO have battled over the "right" amount.) It seems common-sensical that a requirement for being a "money" professional would be sanity regarding money. We need a healthy dose of "Physician, heal thyself" in our industry.[196] The hopeful sign is that firms like CCWM are trailblazing new paths in this direction. They are exploring ways to help people have a healthy relationship to life, and knowing that money is only one element in that journey.

A word on the institutional side of intermediaries, the consultants. They also can play an important role with their clients, if they can abide by the fiduciary standards. Unfortunately (for example), the consultant often plays the role of an insurance policy for pension trustees. Pension trustees can say to regulators, "Look, we hired a reputable consultant to help us, so we upheld our fiduciary obligations." This insurance angle allegedly protects the interests of the pension trustees but not necessarily the plan's beneficiaries. The consultants, motivated by career risk, can be all too willing to avoid the tough conversations with their clients. One prominent example: Consultants should recommend reasonable actuarial return assumptions to the trustees, despite knowing that doing so would materially hurt the plan's "public"-funded status. Another example: Consultants are in the perfect position to help trustees overcome bad decision making when it involves hiring "hot" or firing "cold" asset managers. Consultants can bring educated and objective counsel. They can encourage trustees to stick with an asset manager which is delivering on its promise – the agreed-upon strategy mandate – despite any short-term underperformance. All too often trustees want to fire underperforming managers (sell low) and hire others when they're outperforming (buy high.) Consultants can be the voice of reason that helps avoid these very costly, emotional decisions. That service is valuable and should be prominent in the value proposition of consultants. FCG thinks that instead, too many consultants, like active managers, often sell their "active" selection processes (managers versus securities). Research on the effectiveness of these services indicates that consultants are not adding much value in this regard.[197] The most recent study in the *Journal of Finance* looks at the recommendations for U.S. actively managed equity funds by consultants and concludes, "There is no evidence that these recommendations add value."[198] Like all participants in the New Era, consultants must take a hard look at their value proposition and deliver on it.

Summary:

* Intermediaries – advisors and consultants – can play a vital role in the delivery of value to clients.

* Advisors should become the calm and sane voice that helps people save and invest wisely.

* This role of being the sane voice involves much more emotional intelligence (EQ) than IQ.

* New models are emerging for wealth managers who take a holistic view of the client, rather than emphasizing just the performance.

* Consultants can also offer value-added services if they resist the temptation to placate clients, due to career risk of offering unpopular advice.

* Both advisors and consultants will need to examine their value propositions in the New Era so that they are delivering truly useful services.

---

[190] Ellis, *Index Revolution*, pp. 128 129.

[191] Dan Goleman's book, *Emotional Intelligence* (New York: Bantam Books, 2005) is a good place to start. FCG has been training investment professionals for years on these skills.

[192] Twist, *Soul of Money*, p. xxi.

[193] Ibid., pp. 17 18.

[194] http://www.consciouscapitalwm.com/team/lawrence-ford

[195] Lawrence Ford, personal telephone communication, December 20, 2016.

[196] Luke 4:23. This just means that before attempting to correct others, make sure that you aren't guilty of the same faults.

[197] For two papers on this assertion, see Stewart, Neumann, Knittel, & Heisler, "Absence of Value: An Analysis of Investment Allocation Decisions by Institutional Plan Sponsors," *FAJ* (November/December 2009); Goyal, Amit, & Sunil Wahal, "The Selection and Termination of Investment Management Firms by Plan Sponsors," *Journal of Finance* 63(4) (August 2008), pp. 1805–1847.

[198] Tim Jenkinson, Howard Jones, & Jose Vicente Martinez, "Picking Winners? Investment Consultants' Recommendations of Fund Managers (Digest Summary)," *Journal of Finance* 71(5) (October 2016), pp. 2333 2370; http://www.cfapubs.org/doi/full/10.2469/dig.v47.n3.7

CHAPTER FOURTEEN

Summary: Thinking with New Mindsets

So, where have we arrived on this money, meaning, and mindset journey? How can the investment industry shed its distrusted image and gain a respectable one, based on the profession as a "noble calling"? How does the industry attain a stature such that all of us, as parents, would proudly say to our children, "I hope you will consider a career in the investment industry because we are really helping to make the world a better place"? The argument shouldn't be hard to make. Given the important role of finances in our lives, we should be able to make this statement to our children. Our finances, like our health, are hugely important to our well-being, to our "pursuit of happiness."

Let's review the arguments that we've laid out.

To start with, we argued that the investment world largely – though not exclusively – has an ORANGE mindset. ORANGE does not primarily focus on everyday issues like the happiness of ordinary people. It is much more fascinated by complexities, winning the super-challenging game of investing, and reaping the financial riches of success. Nowadays, though, as the theory of spiral dynamics would predict, ORANGE is proving unable to meet all the demands of the New Era, and GREEN and YELLOW are emerging. GREEN is especially interested in the well-being of all people. Like the Gates Foundation, which is based on the principle that "all people are equal," GREEN thinks more about the well-being of ordinary people, everywhere. GREEN wishes to connect the dots between finance and the common man or woman. Well-being or happiness must replace the abstract goals of benchmarks, alpha, smart beta, and the like.

The crisis in the investment industry – scarce alpha, fee pressures and shrinking margins, shifts from active to passive – provides a powerful catalyst to rethink how things are done. These industry pressures, plus the two outside catalysts of millennials and aging baby boomers, provide additional forces for change. A heightened awareness of purpose, defined as making a positive difference, is driving ORANGE firms to move toward GREEN and YELLOW.

The emergence of these new mindsets helps to illuminate the blindspots in the bright ORANGE approach: too much focus on self-interest, growth, complexity, and shareholder maximization. For all its glorious gifts, bright ORANGE has significant blindpots concerning ethics, clients, value propositions, and reward structures. The fox has been watching the henhouse, and now the clucking of the hens is being heard! Another analogy that we introduced is the "casino mentality." This analogy for the industry compares consumers of investment services to Las Vegas vacationers, who spend time gambling at the casinos. Some will win, most will lose, and the house will always win. The investment industry is the house. It actively encourages people to buy "products" like mutual funds and "win big" rather than to do prudent and patient planning and saving, as markets provide compounding interest over time. The latter approach allows all investors to win over time.

A new leadership mindset, YELLOW, is a hopeful sign for the future. YELLOW is equipped to handle the unprecedented challenges of our times. There are two major reasons why YELLOW can do this:

1. YELLOW operates mostly from a fearless position, with a clear head that is unclouded by emotional drama (greed and fear).
2. YELLOW appreciates all the previous mindsets: RED, BLUE, ORANGE, and GREEN. YELLOW does not think, "I see the world correctly, whereas all of you are biased. Or worse yet, just plain stupid!" There are indications that YELLOW leaders are emerging in the world. The book *Firms of Endearment* describes the characteristics of YELLOW companies and their leaders.

FCG has worked with asset managers who display YELLOW in their leadership. It's encouraging to see that the way forward is not relegated to abstract theory, but actually exists in the world. Firms are embracing the strengths of all the mindsets and combining them in powerful ways to succeed at providing happiness for all their stakeholders.

Not only entire firms, but some investment teams at asset management firms are operating with the full spectrum of mindsets, which allows them to outperform in the markets. ORANGE has a legitimate role in the success and integrity of the investment profession. Nevertheless, FCG's research shows that ORANGE is made better when it teams with the strengths of BLUE and GREEN. Hard and soft skills combined is a winning approach – especially when there is some YELLOW to lead them.

The myopic view that there is one, and only one, way to invest (namely risk/return tradeoffs) is giving way to the view that "values" could drive investment activity. People are driven by their values, so as investment firms figure out ways to package values into attractive portfolios – such as ESG, gender, or Firms of Endearment companies – consumers may find more meaning in investing. They can still earn competitive returns, but in the future, they could get a double win: money *and* meaning, aligned with their mindsets.

As the industry re-examines its value proposition, with a realistic eye toward what actually adds value for clients, we may see enormous shifts in the investment landscape. We may see a lot of the 60% of industry resources now tied up in pursuit of alpha released to help clients achieve more financial well-being. The caveat, of course, is the ORANGE drive for money. Many ORANGE leaders talk a good game about "more GREEN" and so on, but when it comes to less growth and profits, they balk. For example, the overall direction identified by this book is for more CFAs to use their tools in the arena of financial advising: that is, helping mom and pop plan for retirement with realistic, sometimes "boring" portfolios. (Michael Falk on our team coined the phrase: "First immunize, before you even try to optimize." In other words, create a retirement plan that provides a good standard of living and lock it in [immunize], then use any additional funds to attempt further gains [optimize].) Advisor careers are far less monetarily remunerative than Wall Street analyst roles. We may see industry leaders pay lip service to the suggestions in this book, but when push comes to shove, the popular view will be: "Great ideas. Why don't *you* start doing these things! Over here? We'll continue with business as usual!" Unfortunately for them, "business as usual" has changed forever.

The critical role of the intermediary – the financial advisor – offers an important value-add. Financial advisors can be the "money therapists" who help people establish a healthy and sane relationship to money. First, financial advisors – really, all intermediaries – must develop their own healthy relationship to money. Then they can advise clients on what is involved in achieving it for themselves. Consultants also offer important services, *if* they can avoid the temptation to simply placate clients with "safe and friendly" advice.

Based on our view of the investment industry, and the new mindsets that are emerging, we suggest that the graphic shown in Figure 7.1, at the end of Chapter 7, would change in the following ways:

• The investment industry would rise to the top of the Edelman Trust Barometer.

- The industry mindsets would shift to reflect more of a "service" mentality rather than a competitive one. ORANGE would still be core to active managers, but intermediaries would be more GREEN and YELLOW to reflect the service mindset.

- A much smaller portion of the industry's resources (30%) would be aimed at alpha creation.

- Most investment professionals would move up Maslow's hierarchy, realizing that they've met the "deficiency needs" and can now aspire to the "growth needs" at the top. Less fear and Ego-driven behavior, more Higher Self.

- The focus of mission/vision statements would expand to include all stakeholders: clients, employees, owners, and society.

Figure 14.1 Investment Management Ecosystem – Future: 2027

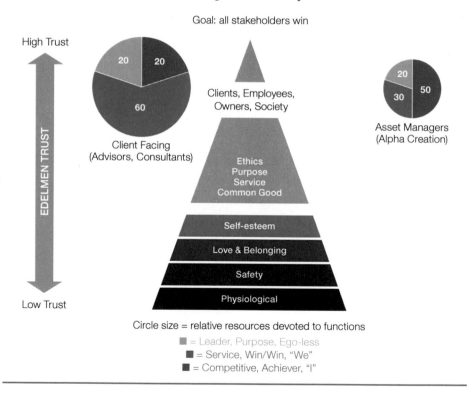

CHAPTER FIFTEEN

Conclusion: Our Vision for Asset Management

L et's return to the simple premise of this book: happiness. For the investment industry to be a noble calling, it must contribute to the well-being and happiness of ordinary citizens. It must address the retirement crisis. People who work hard must be helped and guided by the professionals who understand saving and investing. The fiduciary responsibility must be taken seriously. In the research for this book, we've spoken to many people about their finances and confirmed that the reported low levels of financial literacy are accurate: The average person simply doesn't understand the basics of investing. Can they learn? Should they learn? Of course. But their need creates a wonderful opportunity for investment professionals to be of service in a powerful way. The investment professionals that we've met in our 20 years of serving the industry strongly endorse Schweitzer's quote:

> *I don't know what your destiny will be, but one thing I know: the only ones among you who will be really happy are those who will have sought and found how to serve.*[199]

This is a powerful win/win for both parties: the investment professionals who are privileged to serve and the clients who need the help. Wealth care providers and health care providers are both crucial to people's happiness. Could we adopt our own version of the Hippocratic Oath, part of which reads:

> *May I always act so as to preserve the finest traditions of my calling and may I long experience the joy of healing those who seek my help.*[200]

Can we take the spirit of this oath and re-word it for the investment profession?

> *May I always act so as to preserve the finest traditions of my calling and may I long experience the joy of helping those who seek my advice.*

It is a joy to serve, to help others. Maslow understood this core desire. As Maslow aged – like the baby boomers in the investment world – he added another level to his hierarchy, which he called Self-transcendence. He described it this way:

> The self only finds its actualization in giving itself to some higher goal outside oneself, in altruism and spirituality.[201]

In this definition, Maslow is moving to the collective. Not just me, my team, or my firm, but a natural evolution to a more generous and altruistic mindset. We want to make a difference. We become less Ego-driven and more Higher Self-driven. As wealth care providers we begin to think, "How can our industry provide financial peace of mind for all citizens? How can we contribute to the common good?" This is not fantasy. FCG has met many investment leaders who share this Self-transcendent goal of generosity, altruism, and giving back.[202]

Csikszentmihalyi, author of *Flow*, states:

> One cannot lead a life that is truly excellent without feeling that one belongs to something greater and more permanent than oneself.[203]

Investment professionals who find both passion and purpose in their work naturally experience more happiness. The investment profession offers an ideal calling to do just that: marry passion to purpose. Suzanne Duncan and CFA Institute show this clearly in their research on "phi," just as Dan Pink does in his research on motivation. Finding a larger purpose, a way to make a difference is what truly brings joy:

> Those who do so in the service of some greater objective can achieve even more. The most deeply motivated people – not to mention those who are most productive and satisfied – hitch their desires to a cause larger than themselves.[204]

The Vision

The first step in such a journey is an inspiring vision. Second is a willingness to embrace Einstein's advice: shift our mindsets. Things do change when mindsets change. Remember, there was a time when women were denied the vote, when apartheid was tolerated, and when the Berlin Wall would never come down. The investment industry would do well to think bigger about our purpose. Think beyond making the rich even richer, or developing yet another arcane financial tool, toward declaring that our purpose is improving the financial well-being of people on the planet. Long after the authors of this book have passed on, it would be wonderful to imagine an assessment of our industry that reads like this:

The investment industry has now achieved a proud position in the world. Far from being the lowest ranked industry following the Global Financial Crisis, we are now viewed as the most trusted industry by Edelman. It has been a long journey, but our steadfast commitment to serving all our stakeholders and to seriously embracing the meaning and practice of integrity, has won out over the greed and fear that once characterized our industry. As an industry that is filled with good-hearted, bright people, we have harnessed our skills to help many people achieve a level of financial well-being. And while a small portion of our professionals still compete rigorously to set fair prices and make markets efficient, a much larger percentage of our professionals see themselves as service-minded, genuinely devoted to the financial welfare of clients. We are proud that our industry has grown beyond the zero-sum mindset that assumes some firm's clients will win while others will lose, to an abundance mentality that uses the power of compound interest and upwardly trending markets to make all investors better off over the long term. Additionally, investment professionals have outgrown the belief that the only purpose of a business is to make a profit. Instead, they recognize that the purpose of a firm is to provide goods and services that are valued: in short, to do something useful, for which others are happy to pay. Investors have also outgrown the short-term focus that looks quarter-to-quarter and have embraced the long-term perspective that allows firms to operate optimally. This focus on the long term allows both clients and their investment firms to consider issues like sustainability, social welfare, and the common good as they choose where to allocate resources. Finally, leadership has learned that a major value-add is the development of talent. Leaders are creating cultures that emphasize both purpose and passion, and enable staff members to do their best work and continuously improve. Compensation discussions have become "rewards discussions" in which leaders focus on intrinsic motivators, such as autonomy, mastery, and purpose. Years ago, these notions would have been considered idealistic and even foolish, but the investment industry refuses to settle for simple wins, choosing instead the more challenging "double victory" that both creates profit and increases well-being on the planet. The investment industry has matured and now balances growth and profit with integrity and sustainability. They now aspire to do good and to do well.

The right question to ask as you read this vision is not, "Could this ever really happen?" but rather, "Is it a worthy vision?"

Does it inspire pride in our work and our profession as we contemplate this future? We may not know all the steps to get from here to there, but the vision rallies us to try. At FCG, we simply don't see a downside to embracing this vision. Our sincere hope is that this message touches the hearts and minds of investment leaders and inspires them to begin the journey.

---

[199] https://www.brainyquote.com/quotes/quotes/a/albertschw133001.html

[200] http://guides.library.jhu.edu/c.php?g=202502&p=1335759

[201] *Ibid.*

[202] For the names and firms of such individuals, see FCG's paper, *Linking Culture to Long Term Success* at our website: www.focuscgroup.com

[203] Mihaly Csikszentmihalyi, *Flow* (New York: Harper Perennial Modern Classics, 2008), p. 131.

[204] Pink, *DRIVE*, p. 123.

APPENDIX 1

More ORANGE Aid

Michael Falk, CFA, CRC

B efore expanding on earlier points in the book, let's quickly review. Fair competition (no cheating, Mr. Madoff!) among qualified active investors helps make markets more efficient, and more efficient markets help lead to better allocations of capital.[205] This in turn should better fulfill society's interests. I write "should" because "in theory, there is no difference between theory and practice, but in practice, there is."[206] One practice that makes zero sense is closet indexing (nonactive active management). However, in practice, these portfolios do exist, though they do not increase market efficiency and are mostly a tax on investors. If we're going to return the investment profession to nobility, then perhaps a good first step would be to discontinue the practice of closet indexing?[207] Active investing has value, when active. And qualified investors – those who are largely ORANGE – are needed to execute their craft and compete to bring that value.

We can and should question how much active investing is necessary to help market efficiency, and by association how much ORANGE is necessary. Then again, just as Maslow taught us about how we can *evolve*, the evolution of technology (e.g., robo-advisers and artificial intelligence[208]) may change the question about how much ORANGE will be needed. Paul Tudor Jones has said "No man is better than a machine. And no machine is better than a man with a machine." I agree that the combination of both could be as good as it gets with decision making. However, far fewer ORANGE analysts may be needed, and the remaining talent will have to change their game to be more GREEN and YELLOW. Machines discover and calculate better than humans, but they don't ask questions or dream. The investment business is largely decision making about the future and goals; you have to be able to ask questions and dream.

I think Suzanne Duncan had it spot-on when she wrote "the person *is* the benchmark." More specifically, I think a person's *goals* are the benchmark. Are people and their investments tracking toward their goals? Of course, there are some people whose only goal is to make more money, but that is the vast minority and Ego-based. C'mon, rise above that Maslovian level, you can do it! Sovereign wealth funds are an interesting exception given that they just want to grow the assets – except that their purpose has been argued to be mainly about safeguarding assets for future generations, by getting them out of the current government's hands.

Investing can help you reach your goal(s) more easily. In terms of the blue line in Figure A1.1, the steeper that line is (more risk assets), the smoother (lower-risk or better diversified assets) the "ride" and the easier it is to reach a goal. In turn, if risk assets are expected to provide lower returns, then more savings would be needed or goals would be achieved more slowly, if at all. For example, risk assets today are not expected to produce double-digit returns as they historically did. In fact, the 7% shown in the illustration is arguably still too high (and why the underfunded public pension plan problem is even worse than thought, since their assumptions are typically higher than 7%). Promised (Madoff et al.) or even expected (pension trustees and actuaries) returns that never materialize factor into why our industry has "earned" its reputation, and why a new vision for the industry is needed.

Figure A1.1 Financial Success Path

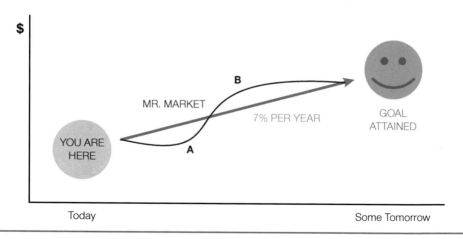

It's all about four and a half steps and how to help clients take them, regardless of whether the goal is to pay for college, buy a house, afford an individual retirement, or fund a pension plan. Each of the four steps is reviewed here. Note: Investment managers benefit from financial adviser and consultant (FAC) intermediaries.

Step 1. Clearly define your goals: when and how much

"If you don't know where you're going, any road'll take you there."[209] The first step is to know where you're going so you know how to get there; that is, which investments can best help to get you there. This step is about the "prize," the purpose of your saving and investing efforts, *not* whether you beat the market, and should be redefined over time as need be.

Step 2. How much to save to, then invest

Saving is a tradeoff: the tradeoff for consumption today versus some tomorrow; a latte today versus weeks of lattes when you retire. If someone is lower on Maslow's scale, saving can be much more difficult. The two key questions to answer are: (a) How much saving is needed to reach the goal based on return expectations; and (b) How much saving is affordable given one's spending? Sometimes goals have to be redefined when return expectations are too low or savings are too few.

Step 3. How to diversify the investments

Yes, Warren Buffet said, "Diversification is protection against ignorance. It makes little sense if you know what you are doing." However, he has also commented on the wisdom of investing in an S&P 500 Index (a diversified, equity index of American companies). So, because most people don't have Buffett's skills (or access to the types of private deals he does), let's diversify. The key questions are: (a) What investments provide useful diversification, and (b) How much should be allocated in the various investments? For example, Treasury bonds offer more diversification with stocks than high-yield bonds, so maybe don't invest in high-yield bonds. Next, how much should be invested in Treasury bonds versus stocks in consideration of the goal(s)? As the market shifts the allocations to Treasuries and stocks over time (e.g., too much in stocks versus Treasuries), when/how should you sell stocks and buy bonds to rebalance[210] the portfolio back to the original allocation strategy, again in consideration of the goal(s)?

Step 4. How to manage Mr. Market's[211] moods (and yours too)

Counseling clients on their temperament (EQ) and their relationship to money and investing is among the most challenging but valuable tasks. Since financial advisers and consultants (FACs) are people too, how's their temperament? In Figure A1.1, Mr. Market experienced both a depressive state ("A") and a manic state ("B"), as he's prone to do. Consider the following situational choices, and never take your eyes off your prized goal:

- In the depressive "A" state, would the client (you?) choose to: (i) rebalance into the underperforming stocks to take advantage of the buying opportunity; (ii) save more, now's the time to buy; (iii) sell the loser stocks and regret their original investment decision; (iv) delay/change the goal; or (v) do nothing?

- In the manic "B" state, would the client (you?) choose to: (i) rebalance into the (safe) Treasuries due to outperformance of the stocks; (ii) take the opportunity to save less; (iii) stay the course, or (iv) accelerate/change the goal?

- Recognize that if the clients (you?) immunized before they tried to optimize, Mr. Market's moods would not disrupt their goal (or their stress level.)

Step 4.5. How to leverage time

Albert Einstein told us: "Compound interest is the eighth wonder of the world. He who understands it, earns it." So, can you save/invest early and remain invested over time? This is as much about whether other savings (or insurance) exist for short-term or emergency needs as it is about temperament. Of course, temperament is inescapable: will you stay invested when Mr. Market is depressed, and depresses you?

The often largely ORANGE FACs and IMs each can play valuable roles with the four and a half steps. However, do they? This is not about skill, but rather will. Value can often be telling clients what they may not wish to hear or to do something that's uncomfortable. Does ORANGE (or anyone else) embrace career risks of doing the "right" thing, or do they simply do what the client wishes? Then again, isn't giving the clients what they want the right thing to do? This raises appropriate but uncomfortable questions for clients, their FACs and IMs. It also highlights the fact that the client is part of the system.

FACs could execute four and a half steps and allocate the remaining assets for growth … among IMs who would invest the dollars they were given. Of course, the client may choose to go directly to the investment manager and perform the intermediary tasks herself. Fine, good. Got financial literacy? That leads to another defined, significant value – which is less ORANGE and more GREEN – in education. Clients can and do count on their FACs to help educate them. However, once again, this could be a fox watching the henhouse. So, how about requiring financial literacy education in middle and high schools, to help the hens of the future, if only to better understand which FACs to work with?

The Cost of ORANGE(s) and the Price of Scarcity Mentalities

The industry and its players' potential value is evident, but at what price? Or is it the other way around? Oscar Wilde told us long ago that "people know the price of everything and the value of nothing."[212] Earlier in the book, we shared how assessing the value of stuff, like an iPhone or car, may not be that difficult. It's far more difficult with investments and financial services because the value will not be known until some point in the future when the decision(s) helped your clients reach their goals or failed to. Ugh! Somehow the axiom "you pays you money and you takes your chances" just doesn't seem fair[213] – which it doesn't in more and more clients' eyes; hence the massive flows out of actively managed portfolios and into cheap, cheap index portfolios.[214] We would like to define *fair* as a win/win/win for the clients, FACs, and IMs. After all, services are being provided (is not the financial *services* industry a service industry at its core?) as well as being demanded. Let's begin with understanding the demand side before thinking about the suppliers:

The Client

At first blush, this seems to be about financial literacy. If clients are savvy, then maybe there would be far less demand. Maybe, but that perspective is incomplete. The complexity of regulation(s) and the breadth of product areas is enough,[215] for many, to still preserve some demand. First and foremost, clients need to ask themselves: (1) how much time do they have to think about or do planning/investing; (2) how much interest do they have in spending time on planning/investing; and (3) how much knowledge or interest in learning about planning/investing do they have?

How much a client "should" pay ought to depend on the services needed and a competitive marketplace (hopefully). So, how is the competitive marketplace pricing services, and how should it?

The FACs

The competitive marketplace is evolving today, and rapidly. Robo-advisers, for example, may or may not be able to replicate all the services of the good financial advisers, but they're trying, they're evolving rapidly, and they're cheap. Their low asset-based fees are hard to beat. Regardless, going back to the "how to" four and a half steps, there's clearly value-add potential for the FACs. Maybe surprisingly, the number of similarities between FAs and consultants, from the perspective of the steps, is significant. Consultants get paid retainer (hourly-styled) fees because asset-based fees on their sizable accounts would otherwise seem … rude.[216] So, why wouldn't the FAs also get paid retainer or hourly fees for their efforts, since their services are like those of the consultants? Also, "because their accounts are smaller," smaller fees seem somewhat logical. Of course, how they charge (hourly versus asset-based versus asset-based with a cap) isn't as important as the total, billable amount for services. This is about the setting the price of ORANGE(s).

Now for a reality check: Clients often choose traditional (noncapped) asset-based fees from their financial advisers instead of "writing a check." Behaviorally, they're more comfortable paying in this passive manner, especially when it's a higher amount. Financial literacy does explain this; clients are part of the system. However, what's important is the total cost, and clients are the final arbiters of value.

IMs

If there's such a thing as ORANGE "juice," then it's with the IMs. Asset-based fees are part of their DNA and the business. This doesn't make it right, but this is an industry in which additional competition hasn't historically hurt profit margins. Not good. However, today, clients are voting with their feet and buying index funds. Moreover, competition is changing, with more and better quantitative techniques that are priced more cheaply (think computers/technology versus people.) In this New Era, IMs are experiencing margin compression as never before, but not those who have been adding value. In short, many ORANGEs are being squeezed – and, maybe, that's okay. The actively managed, "classic" IMs get, for example, 0.80% on the equity assets they manage, win or lose. How can a win-or-lose proposition ever be a win/win?

What if IMs grew some GREEN and pursued a win/win proposition that wouldn't hurt their business's sustainability? It's possible with what the industry today calls "fulcrum fees."[217] Here is a fulcrum approach along with optional features all of which could lead to a win/win structure:

1. **The Fulcrum Approach.** The IM would get a small, beta-like, base fee (e.g., 30 basis points), and a performance fee (e.g., 30% of alpha earned) based on the level of benchmark "plus" performance he or she generated. Of course, the time period and benchmark should be mutually agreed upon in advance with the client. Regardless of whether an IM always wins, they do have the expenses of their business and you would be getting service, but when/if they win so would the client net of all fees. Some firms today[218] offer zero base fees or refund fees in the event of actual losses. Both approaches are obviously win/win; however, if an IM doesn't have a sustainable business, then that win/win could lose. Such approaches, once time (bear market) tested, might make for nice features but seem uncertainly sustainable until proven otherwise.

2. **A Feature.** The IM/client could add a "high watermark" such that there could be no performance fee after any subbenchmark results until the benchmark was again exceeded.

3. **A Feature.** In lieu of a benchmark, the IM/client could have a "hurdle rate" feature in which performance fees would be zero until a threshold return (e.g., inflation + 4%) was earned.

The real question is what percentage of IMs today could run their business off a 30 basis point fee? The high rates of compensation for so many of the best/brightest ORANGEs play into the scarcity mentality. BUT, c'mon: they're not at risk of standing in any soup lines! To pursue this win/win, an IM's operations would have to be priced off the base fee only and not any assumed performance fees; if not, then that IM's business may not be sustainable. Sustainability is necessary.

All this describes a win/win, being of service to clients, sustainability, and being of value across the primary players. That's the New Era to me: a card-carrying member of the ORANGE mindset.

---

205 Conversely, without active investors, markets would be less efficient and the efficacy of capital allocation would be harmed.

206 Attributed to Yogi Berra, famed NY Yankee Hall-of-Fame catcher.

207 David Ricketts, "Swedish Regulator Names Closet-Tracker Funds," *Financial Times* (January 7, 2017). However, the "watchdog still has no official definition of index-hugging products," and what will come of them remains a question.

208 Furthermore, as AI continues to advance (Nathaniel Popper, "The Robots Are Coming for Wall Street," *New York Times* (February 25, 2016), https://www.nytimes.com/2016/02/28/magazine/the-robots-are-coming-for-wall-street.html?_r=0), the ORANGE roles, in terms of analysts, are becoming threatened.

209 A paraphrase of an exchange between Alice and the Cheshire Cat in Lewis Carroll's *Alice's Adventures in Wonderland.*

210 I was quoted in an interesting debate on this topic; see Robert Powell, "Portfolio Rebalancing Might Be Overrated," Wall Street Journal (January 9, 2017); http://www.wsj.com/articles/portfolio-rebalancing-might-be-overrated-1483931101

211 Ben Graham's fictional, bipolar personality (from depressive to manic) of the market.

212 Quoted in Wilde's play, *Lady Windermere's Fan.*

213 Unless, of course, you like gambling and casinos have entertainment value (and free drinks).

214 Note that this does *not* necessarily include index portfolios offered for free. Free in this case might be too expensive, because the investment manager's profits come from lending out your securities, a strategy that has different potential risks/costs.

215 Michael is a good example. He is a CFA, CRC, taught CFP classes and uses some IMs as well as consults with a CFP, CPA, and estate planning lawyer from time to time.

216 Maybe *rude* isn't the right word, but does this make OCIOs ORANGE by definition, because many are consultants or consultant firms who wanted asset-based fees?

217 Jason Zweig, "A Fee Structure for Fund Managers Who Put Their Money Where Their Mouth Is," *Wall Street Journal* (January 11, 2017); http://blogs.wsj.com/moneybeat/2017/01/11/a-fee-structure-for-fund-managers-who-put-their-money-where-their-mouth-is/

218 *Ibid.*

APPENDIX 2

Phi-Agnostic Survey from State Street/CFA Institute

State Street Research has developed a survey to measure "phi" in an organization. Phi has been shown to provide motivation for investment professionals, thereby raising engagement and performance. Throughout this paper we have referenced Suzanne Duncan and her team's work. If you wish to explore the phi diagnostic for your organization, please contact Liz Severyns at lseveryns@focuscgroup.com. The survey methodology is described here.

Survey Methodology
Primary research for this study included a survey of 6938 respondents across 20 countries. State Street Center for Applied Research partnered with CFA Institute in this research effort.

Participating institutional investors include government pension funds, corporate pension funds, retail pension plans, sovereign wealth funds, central banks, insurance firms, healthcare institutions, endowments, and foundations. Participating retail investors include mass market, mass affluent, and high-net-worth individuals. Participating asset managers include institutional-oriented asset managers, retail-oriented asset managers, blend retail/institutional asset managers (more retail-oriented) and blend retail/institutional asset managers (more institutional-oriented). Participating intermediaries include bank/broker-affiliated advisors, institutional consultants, independent financial advisors, and insurance-affiliated advisors. Public entities include regulatory bodies and government officials, as well as policymakers with a focus on financial services-related policy matters.

FCG has teamed with State Street and CFA Institute (authors of the Phi study) to administer the survey and consult on the results. For more on this offering contact Liz Severyns at lseveryns@focusCgroup.com

The questions used to calculate phi for professionals are listed below, with the option indicating higher phi marked in bold and weighted equally in the phi score.

(On purpose) What motivates you to perform generally and in your current role? (Select top three)

a) The hope of receiving a big bonus/salary increase.

b) The fact that everyone can see my performance and I do not want to look bad.

c) I know it is important to fulfill the end client's goals.

d) **The feeling of doing something in the service of something larger than myself (e.g., creating a better life situation for the end client, supporting the values of my organization to achieve long-term organizational growth).**

e) I just love what I do and would continue doing it even if I was not paid.

(On habits) What is the reason that you are still working in the investment management industry? (Select up to two)

a) I am reasonably satisfied with my job.

b) It is where the money is, i.e. where I can earn the most.

c) I like the status that a job in this industry brings.

d) I am passionate about the markets.

e) I am inspired by a family member/industry figure.

f) **I can help people and organizations achieve their financial goals.**

g) I like working with very smart people.

h) **I help facilitate economic growth and development.**

i) It would be too difficult to change jobs and pursue a new career in another industry.

j) I am thinking about quitting.

(On incentives) Which description most closely matches the way you think about your work?

a) As a job (I work only for the sake of the money, I am really happy when the weekend comes and I satisfy my intellectual curiosity and interests via hobbies and not work.)

b) As a career (My work energizes me, and my aim is to advance and get promoted. I sometimes bring work home with me because I want to deliver excellent results. Sometimes I do, however, wonder about the meaning and importance of what I do.)

c) As a calling (I am devoted to my work. When working, I feel that I am part of something larger than myself. The value my efforts bring is clear to me and I never question the meaning of what I do. I would continue to work even if I was independently wealthy.)

APPENDIX 3

Focus Elite Firms

2015

1. AJO, Philadelphia, PA*
2. American Beacon Advisors, Irving, TX*
3. Disciplined Growth Investors, Minneapolis, MN*
4. Forest Investment Associates, Atlanta, GA
5. Kempen Capital Management, Amsterdam, The Netherlands
6. Lighthouse Partners, Palm Beach Gardens, FL
7. Mawer Investment Management Ltd., Calgary, Alberta, Canada
8. Roehl & Yi Investment Advisors, LLC, Eugene, OR

2014

1. AJO, Philadelphia, PA
2. American Beacon Advisors, Fort Worth, TX
3. Disciplined Growth Investors, Minneapolis, MN
4. Forest Investment Associates, Atlanta, GA
5. Greystone Managed Investments, Inc., Regina, Saskatchewan, Canada
6. Kempen Capital Management, Amsterdam, The Netherlands
7. Mawer Investment Management Ltd., Calgary, Alberta, Canada
8. Roehl & Yi Investment Advisors, LLC, Eugene, OR
9. XYZ Capital (anonymous), East Coast

2013

1. AJO, Philadelphia, PA
2. American Beacon Advisors, Fort Worth, TX
3. Disciplined Growth Investors, Minneapolis, MN
4. Forest Investment Associates, Atlanta, GA
5. Greystone Managed Investments, Inc., Regina, Saskatchewan, Canada
6. Kempen Capital Management, Amsterdam, The Netherlands
7. Mawer Investment Management, Ltd., Calgary, Alberta, Canada
8. XYZ Capital (anonymous), East Coast

2011

1. AJO
2. Disciplined Growth Investors
3. Forest Investment Associates
4. Retirement Advisors of America
5. Greystone Managed Investments, Inc.
6. ABC Capital (anonymous), East Coast

* These firms are considered Super Elite as they have earned the distinction at least three consecutive years and have a sludge factor under 4%.

APPENDIX 4

Additional Focus Elite Firms

A dditional Focus Elite firms are described briefly here. They each display the same mindsets that are highlighted in Appendix 3 on Elite firms. For more on these firms, see our white paper, *Culture and Success*, on our website.

American Beacon Advisors (Irving, TX)

Strong leadership is required to design and develop strong culture. American Beacon Advisors (ABA) is fortunate to have two such leaders, Gene Needles and Jeff Ringdahl. In our 360 assessment work with ABA, these leaders each scored the highest ratings FCG has ever seen. We usually highlight a leader's top five scores from a list of 60 competency factors, scored on a 5 point scale. In this way, leaders gain insight about which competencies are strong and, therefore, should be leveraged. In the case of Gene and Jeff, there leadership scores were so high (4.9 on the 5 scale), that we listed 25 and 26 competencies respectively for them! It's no wonder that ABA's culture has been a perennial Focus Elite winner. And that the firm has achieved excellent success on many traditional measures.

American Beacon Advisors has not only become the top sub-advisor mutual fund company but has also been able to, under Gene and Jeff's leadership, buck the overall trend of active asset management industry as a whole. While the industry has been in negative sales since mid-2011 and had it worst period in Q3 2016, American Beacon was able to record $450M in net flows in 2016. In 2016, they closed on the firm's first two outside acquisitions (a minority interest in ARK Investment Management LLC; a majority interest in Alpha Quant Advisors) as well as acquiring a majority interest in Shapiro Capital Management in early 2017.

Most recently, Gene and Jeff have begun to position the business for the next stage of growth. In 2017, Resolute Investment Managers was created as a multi-affiliate business following the successful acquisitions of ARK, Alpha Quant and Shapiro.

Serving as the parent company focused on acquisitions and oversight of investment affiliates, Resolute is driven by future value creation and is focused on revenue (rather than cost) synergies. Resolute partners with management teams who believe their greatest successes are ahead and can utilize American Beacon Advisors, a cornerstone affiliate of Resolute, as their key distribution, legal, marketing and HR partner.

Below are the culture results for ABA for the last three surveys. These are the top values in the firm, as voted on by the entire staff. Remember that values listed in green are both "existing" (i.e. have) and "aspirational" (i.e. want). In the most recent survey, 2013, their existing and aspirational cultures are nearly identical, which is ideal.

Figure A4.1 Yearly Comparisons: Existing Culture

December 2010 N = 64	April 2012 N = 78	November 2013 N = 84
Ethical/Integrity	Ethical/Integrity	Ethical/Integrity
Client Satisfaction	Professional	Professional
Expense Control	Profit/Financial Success	Balance (Home/Work)
Results Oriented	Collaboration/Teamwork	Collaboration/Teamwork
Professional	Results Oriented	Results Oriented
Profit/Financial Success	Accountability/ Responsibility	Profit/Financial Success
Balance (Home/Work)	Balance (Home/Work)	Long Term Perspective/ Vision
Collaboration/Teamwork	Expense Control	Accountability/ Responsibility
Fast Paced	Shareholder/ Owner Focus	Client Satisfaction
Shareholder/ Owner Focus	Client Satisfaction	Positive

Green = Match between top existing and aspirational values in given year.

Addenda (Montreal/Toronto)

This Canadian firm has been working on culture for a solid decade. Like Greystone, they have turned their leadership team over as well. The factor we want to highlight for Addenda is their laser-like focus on the client. When Mike White was CEO, he would open the "Town Hall" meetings with a PowerPoint photo of a person sitting behind a desk. Mike would ask the staff, "Who is this person?" The response was puzzled expressions. Mike would wait for a few seconds, then answer, "He's your boss! That is one of our clients." As you see in the culture results in Figure A4.2, Addenda's devotion to the client has never wavered.

Figure A4.2 Yearly Comparisons: Existing Culture

May 2010	Nov 2010	Nov 2011	Oct 2013	Jan 2017
Client Satisfaction	Client Satisfaction	Client Satisfaction	Client Satisfaction	Client Satisfaction
Collaboration/ Teamwork	Ethical/ Integrity	Collaboration/ Teamwork	Collaboration/ Teamwork	Balance (Home/Work)
Professional	Balance (Home/Work)	Balance (Home/Work)	Professional	Professional
Ethical/ Integrity	Professional	Ethical/ Integrity	Balance (Home/Work)	Ethical/ Integrity
Balance (Home/Work)	Respect	Professional	Ethical/ Integrity	Collaboration/ Teamwork
Respect	Collaboration/ Teamwork	Long Term Perspective/ Vision	Analytic/ Research Oriented	Long Term Perspective/ Vision
Accountability/ Responsibility	Trust/Sincerity	Respect	Expense Control	Community/ Social Responsibility
Clear Performance Goals	Analytic/ Research Oriented	Results Oriented	Long Term Perspective/ Vision	Competence
Fair	Clear Performance Goals	Loyalty	Results Oriented	Respect
Results Oriented	Fair	Analytic/ Research Oriented	Clear Performance Goals	Results Oriented

Green = Match between top existing and aspirational values in given year.

Kempen (Amsterdam)

Kempen Capital Management is different from the other Elite firms in two ways. Kempen is larger (155 employees) and European (based in the Netherlands and the U.K.). The top value for three surveys running is "professional." And our interviews revealed that this value reflected a deep commitment on their part to ethics, integrity and fiduciary responsibility. In other words, if I am a professional, then I behave in an exemplary manner.

Figure A4.3 Yearly Comparisons: Existing Culture

May 2010 N = 116	February 2013 N = 143
Professional	Professional
Results Oriented	Collaboration/Teamwork
Hands-On/Action-Oriented	Hands-On/Action-Oriented
Commitment	Results Oriented
Client Satisfaction	Client Satisfaction
Intelligent	Passion/Energy/Motivate
Humor/Fun	Excellence/Continuous Improvement
Collaboration/Teamwork	Competitive/Win/Be the Best
Long Hours/Hard Work	Commitment
Entrepreneurial	Entrepreneurial

Green = Match between top existing and aspirational values in given year.

It helps that this Dutch asset manager has a strong culture that puts craftsmanship first when it comes to their professional lives. All want to be the best at their chosen profession and improve all the time. As a result, Kempen consist of a group of professionals who all think that they have the best job in the company. And that, in turn, leads to nice new things. For lack of a better word: let's call it innovation.

Innovation, disruption, they all spark excitement. More than the concept of long-termism: this seems to imply that everything goes, but slowly. The opposite is true: with a long-term engaged shareholder on board, a public company is able to focus on growth, innovation and the change that is needed to keep performance high in the future. The key word is engagement; an investor should have knowledge about what the plans are for the future, and if these plans support long-term goals. At Kempen they have been applying this investment philosophy for 25 years, for instance in all their small-cap strategy.

This way of working attracts people who do not care much for hierarchy and who value autonomy. Making money is important, but being 'top of the class' even more. They make each other better professionals, every day. And the staff invests in their own funds: 'eat your own cooking' as it is called in the financial sector. But what do clients say?

Kempen has a net promotor score of 32% in the last survey they did (2015), climbing from 22% (in 2013). Improvement was seen by 53% of the participants in the level of service. The company had, not surprisingly, high marks for level of expertise and integrity. Empathy is a region where there is room for improvement. Who are their clients? The retired entrepreneur in private banking? The trustee of a pension fund? Or the consultant of the insurance company? The business-to-business client or the pensioner or family office owner with whom it all ends (or starts)? It really doesn't matter that much, because the same thing has to be done for all clients: keep it as simple as possible in a complicated environment.

The financial sector has a tendency to overcomplicate things. This has created a gap between those who know, and those who don't understand. Of course, this happens in every sector that consist of highly educated and very skilled people. It gives you the responsibility of explaining to the public what it is that you do exactly. That is why Lars Dijkstra, the CIO of Kempen wrote in an article: 'We need to transition from short-term salesmanship to long-term stewardship.' He also served as the Chairman of the 300 Club, mentioned earlier in this book, which represents a group of global investment leaders intent on improving the industry. Kempen has also joined a group of companies determined to reduce short-termism: FCLT Global is a not-for-profit organization dedicated to developing practical tools and approaches that encourage long-term behaviors in business and investment decision-making.

An important factor of this stewardship is alignment of interest: the interests of the client, the asset manager and the employees should be aligned. This can be realized by making the senior-employees co-owners of the company and allowing them to invest in their own funds, or: 'Have skin in the game'. Next to this, Kempen is focused: the emphasis lies on a limited number of high quality strategies in the less-efficient parts of financial markets. As they say within Kempen: "We do things well or we don't do them." The third important factor is a strong long-term commitment, both of the clients and the asset manager.

The clients of Kempen face big challenges. To help them face these challenges, we need long-term focused specialists who have clearly tied their interest to those of their clients. A craftsman (or woman) who understands the ultimate need of his client, molded into a modern version of the old profession. They are aware that the future of asset management lies more in delivering and improving real returns, instead of benchmark returns. But there is more. At Kempen they want to become indispensable for clients by delivering in the long run three alphas: a service-alpha, an investment-alpha and an innovation-alpha. Kempen is operating in a fast-changing environment. This requires the ability to adapt quickly, stay agile and above all: maintain a good working environment and secure vitality of the staff; physically as well as mentally.

At Kempen they nurture a new generation of engaged professionals. Young people and very experienced people who all master their trade and want to improve all the time. Not just for bonuses at the end of the year, but to build something of their own and to create value for all stakeholders. Sometimes that building can take years. Because progress can be fast and fun, but more often it takes time and deliberation and, most of all, the courage to be a little bit, or even a lot, different.

In Holland it is important that you don't stand out too much. The prime minister's party even has: "act normal" as its motto. Kempen applauds this humility in the sense that they do not want to overcomplicate things. But, in another way Kempen is out of the ordinary for the Dutch, because of their absolute dedication, how highly selective they are in what they do and for who they do it, with modern craftmanship and an appetite for progress.

And they are not afraid to take it slow.

APPENDIX 5

Typical Agenda for Michael Falk Embedding Assignments

Table A5.1 Embedding Agenda

PRE	n/a	• MF to receive: IPS, process related documents and team org chart
DAY 1	Morning	• Firm product pitch to MF (preferably an investment person and a sales person • Attend an investment committee meeting (as scheduled)
	Afternoon	• Begin team member interviews (30-45 minutes each) • If possible, dinner with key members of the team this evening
DAY 2	Morning	• Complete interview sessions as need be; random conversations as desired • Final preparations for afternoon diagnostic
	Afternoon	• An investment team session to check the team's alignment/ understanding of the firm's philosophy, process and execution (diagnostic included)
DAY 3	Morning	• Meet with IC leadership to dialogue on the team, their processes, their execution and proposed improvements • Prepare for afternoon team session
	Afternoon	• The 2nd investment team session to discuss what has been learned, to test alignment of recommendation thoughts
POST	n/a	• MF to send recommendations report and all embedding diagnostics

APPENDIX 6

Personality Styles and the Spiral Dynamics Framework

Table A6.1 Personality Styles

Spiral Level: Personality style that is similar:	BLUE • Methodical • Practical • Structured • Detail-oriented	ORANGE • Competitive • Focused • Logical • Blunt	GREEN • Collaborative • Relationship • Trust/Respect • Idealistic
Myers-Briggs	Sensing- Thinking- Judging	Intuitive Thinking Judging	Intuitive Feeling
Kiersey Temperament	Guardian	Rationalist	Communalist/Idealist
Competing Values Framework	Hierarchy	Market	Clan
DiSC	Conscientious/Steady	Dominant	Influencer
Business Chemistry Model[219]	Guardians	Drivers	Integrators

---

[219] Suzanne Johnson Vickberg & Kim Christfort, "The New Science of Team Chemistry," *Harvard Business Review* (March/April 2017).

APPENDIX 7

The 21 Skills for Spiritual Intelligence (Cindy Wigglesworth)

C indy Wigglesworth has written an important book that addresses the question, "What is the Higher Self that you've been referring to throughout the book?" She removes all the controversy that religion brings to this discussion and describes the Higher Self in neutral terms. For leaders who aspire to be truly YELLOW, this book is a wonderful resource. She offers trainings and more resources on her website: www.deepchange.com

The 21 skills are as follows.

Know Thyself:

Skill 1:   Awareness of Own Worldview

Skill 2:   Awareness of Life Purpose

Skill 3:   Awareness of Values Hierarchy

Skill 4:   Complexity of Inner Thought

Skill 5:   Awareness of Ego Self/Higher Self

Know the World:

Skill 6:   Awareness of Interconnectedness of Life

Skill 7:   Awareness of Worldviews of Others

Skill 8:   Breadth of Time Perception

Skill 9:   Awareness of Limitations/Power of Human Perception

Skill 10: Awareness of Spiritual Laws

Skill 11: Experience of Transcendent Oneness

Self-Mastery:

Skill 12: Commitment to Spiritual Growth

Skill 13: Keeping Higher Self in Charge

Skill 14: Living Your Purpose and Values

Skill 15: Sustaining Faith

Skill 16: Seeking Guidance from Higher Self

Social Mastery & Spiritual Presence:

Skill 17: Being a Wise and Effective Teacher/Mentor of Spiritual Principles

Skill 18: Being a Wise and Effective Leader/Change Agent

Skill 19: Making Compassionate and Wise Decisions

Skill 20: Being a Calming, Healing Presence

Skill 21: Being Aligned with the Ebb and Flow of Life

About the Authors

James Ware, CFA, founded the Focus Consulting Group in 1999. He has authored three prior books on investing, and numerous articles appearing in *The Financial Analysts Journal, The Journal of Portfolio Management, Harvard Business Review, and CFA Magazine.* He is a frequent speaker at industry events, such as the CFA Annual, the Greenwich Roundtable, the U.S. Delegates CIO Roundtable, and the Financial Analysts Seminar. His academic background is Williams College and the University of Chicago Business School. He lives with his wife and two daughters in Long Grove, Illinois.

Keith Robinson is the Managing Partner of Focus Consulting Group and brings more than 30 years of business and investment experience to his consulting and coaching work at FCG. As an expert in talent management, he has a natural passion for helping firms and individuals play at the top of their game. He is the co-author of various FCG white papers; has published articles on "Managing the Human Portfolio" and "Managing the Millennials"; and been an industry speaker on a variety of investment topics related to talent, culture, and leadership. Keith holds a MBA from University of Illinois and graduated *summa cum laude* with a business degree from Western Connecticut.

Michael Falk, CFA, CRC, is a Partner with the Focus Consulting Group and specializes in helping investment teams with improving their investment philosophy, process, and execution techniques; and investment firms with their strategic planning. He has been a chief strategist on a global macro limited partnership, a CIO in charge of manager due diligence and asset allocation for an institutional multibillion-dollar advisory, and a practicing financial adviser early in his nearly 30-year career. Michael is the author of the CFA Institute Research Foundation Monograph *Let's All Learn How to Fish ... to Sustain Long-Term Economic Growth.* He is also part of the CFA Institute's Approved Speaker List, and teaches on behalf of the CFA Society of Chicago in its "Foundations of Investing" program. In the past, he taught at DePaul University in its Certified Financial Planner (CFP) certificate program.

Focus Consulting Group Services

Serving over 400 clients in 20 countries for nearly 2 decades

OUR MISSION
To help investment leaders succeed by leveraging talent.

OUR APPROACH
*We partner with investment firms to improve their effectiveness
and their ability to add value to stakeholders.*

LEADERSHIP: Increasing leadership effectiveness among self, team, firm

- 360 assessments for strengths, weaknesses, blind spots and development

- Executive coaching and change management

- Team analysis and diagnostics

CULTURE: Building a high performing, learning culture

- Culture analysis, diagnostics and debrief

- Culture management and industry comparison

- Benchmarking to attract and retain talent, improve decision-making

REWARDS AND INCENTIVES: Designing plans that are fair, transparent, and simple

- Industry benchmarks research

- Interviews and discovery of current and preferred reward philosophy

- Design and facilitation of total compensation and incentive plans

INVESTMENT PHILOSOPHY AND PROCESS: Defining and sharpening your team's decision making

- Philosophy and process, and talent assessments

- Leveraging behavioral finance tools and techniques

- Embedding with teams to observe and improve their process and execution

STRATEGY: Moving your firm to its preferred future

- SWOT analysis based on industry expertise
- Discussion and agreement on strategic planning process
- Connecting the strategic plan to responsibilities and your rewards system

SUCCESSION: Putting the right people in the right roles at the right time using a merit-based process

- Developing a talent pipeline
- Assessment of talent and facilitation of talent review
- Process for design and implementation of succession plan

TALENT MANAGEMENT: Managing the three C's approach: competence, contribution, criticality

- Understanding your firm's bench strength
- Managing performance through improved performance reviews and feedback
- Creating development paths for increasing skills, capabilities and performance: learning skills of high-performing investment teams

OFFSITE DESIGN AND FACILITATION: Getting the most from bringing the whole team/firm together

- C-suite or team dynamics, improving the performance through clear goal alignment
- Leadership development via "learning experiences" on various topics, such as better communication and mindfulness
- Increasing team effectiveness and development

COMMUNICATIONS: Boosting the impact of messaging for leaders, teams and client-facing professionals

- Improving team productivity, engagement and effectiveness through communications assessments and development programs
- Leveraging individual style through customized presentation coaching
- Strengthening client and prospect relationships by focusing on clarity, consistency and character in all forms of communication (verbal, written, non-verbal)

For more information about FCG's services, please contact:
Liz Severyns at lseveryns@focuscgroup.com

Index